Dedication

To my dear wife, Barbara, who has shown the preciousness of going the way of true love, again, and again, and again.

Be Fruitful, Multiply, and Take Dominion

A Pathway to Happiness and World Peace

By Stephen Stacey

Part one of the three-blessings series

Copyright © 2020 by Stephen Stacey

All rights reserved. No part of this book may be reproduced, stored into a retrieval system, or transmitted, in any form or by any means, electronic, mechanical, photocopying, recording or otherwise, without the prior permission of the author except in the case of very brief quotations embodied within reviews and certain non-commercial uses permitted by copyright law.

_____

Lovebird Publishing

ISBN: 978-1-9161277-3-9

Contents

FOREWORD	I
1. ARE WE POLAR BEARS OR PUFFINS?	**1**
Are We Polar Bears Or Puffins?	1
The Marital Norms Of The Truelove Species	3
"Mummy And Daddy, Do You Love Me?"	14
Our Truelove Norm Builds Successful Nations	20
Marriage Is A Natural Responsibility	24
2. SOPHIE AND RICHARD HAVE CHILDREN—A CULTURE IS BORN	**27**
Our Marital Norm Creates Cultural Energy	27
The Continued Existence Of A Culture	29
The Marital Family Sustains A Culture	31
The Marital Family And Cultural Development	36
3. THE THREE-BLESSINGS FRAMEWORK	**47**
The Three Ways That Humans Receive Blessings	47
The Inner Workings Of The First And Third Blessing	54
All Religions Seek To Uphold Our Species Norms	58
Social Institutions And Our Species Norm	62
The Natural Rights Of Humans	64
The Story Of Our Humanity	67
4. AN EXPLORATION OF THE THIRD BLESSING	**71**
The Fundamental Rules Of The Third Blessing	71
Singapore Follows A Natural And Sustainable Path	72
Mormonism Shows Us A Faith-Based Model	78
The Social Fabric Through Legislators' Eyes	80
5. ON HUMAN WHOLESOMENESS	**85**
Mind And Body Unity	85
Core Values	88
Love And Beauty	89
The Divine Value Of The Individual	93

6. ONLY PUFFINS CAN BUILD DEMOCRACIES — 101
THE STATE'S INTEREST IN MARRIAGE — 101
NO MARITAL-FAMILY NORM LEADS TO NO DEMOCRACY — 110
NATURAL RIGHTS AND SPECIES NORMS — 112

7. THE ONLY PATH TO WORLD PEACE — 133
THE THREE BLESSINGS OR BUST — 133
ONE DAY, WE WILL WORK IT OUT — 146

FOREWORD

This book did not start out as an attempt to understand how world peace might ultimately come about. Five years ago, I had just stopped teaching a positive psychology course at a university in Finland and wanted to write a book on the self-development model I had created.

Then, one day, I stuck my head out of the forest where I was living to see what the universities in America were doing to improve the emotional and relationship well-being of their students. What I saw left me both shocked and perplexed. Where I taught the value of gratitude, I found numerous courses teaching criticism. Where I taught the ability to look at difficulties as opportunities for growth, I found courses teaching victimhood. And where I taught forgiveness as a means to manage personal well-being, I found textbooks extolling the value of ongoing resentment. If I desired to destroy a country or harm people's lives, these are some of the damaging attitudes I might choose to teach too. But why was a university system seeking to destroy its nation?

Having seen this, my soul could not rest. As is the way with some humans, an inner voice made a demand. "You have to look into what is happening. This is something you have to do." The plea grew more persistent. Eventually, I succumbed.

The process of writing has been the same since the very start. Almost every day, I would wake up with some new thoughts as if my mind was being programmed as I slept. This book is just one of three books that I will publish because of this long thinking process.

In this first book, because of the confusion that I found both within the education system and the wider society, I have been guided to answer a fundamental question. "What kind of worldview would human beings need to adopt if they sincerely wished to build a world of peace, happiness, and co-prosperity?" It took a long time for me to find a firm basis for this solution and consider whether it was the only foundation upon which such a world was possible. If there is only one solution, and if we sincerely desire a peaceful world, then it only makes sense that we head in that direction.

Along with the daily revelations, I was encouraged to take responsibility to look deeply into the research on a variety of issues. I also spent a substantial amount of time listening to the testimonies of various people who felt they had been led down an unhelpful path in life.

Additionally, it helped that I had spent several years previously looking at the data on the marital family and what worked and what did not when it came to the building of a lasting relationship. I believe many readers do not need to be reminded of the importance of the marital family to society's well-being. However, because of this prior knowledge, I decided to highlight this theme as a means to provide the framework upon which the rest of the book is based.

I fully understand that issues surrounding family and sexuality are highly sensitive issues. Thus, some readers might consider me insensitive in the way I express myself. However, my sole intention is to show that, throughout history, various groups of citizens have picked up a set of principles that guided them in their efforts to create thriving nations. Some even built empires because of the level of energy they generated using these principles. And, when these nations started to ignore these principles, they went into decline. Hardships followed.

Based on such an understanding, it is possible to ask some questions. "Might we be able to identify these principles and purposely use them to build flourishing nations?" Also, "Because we understand these principles, might we be able to keep refining them so that decay doesn't set in again?" And lastly, "Because all nations will have access to these principles, might all nations choose to develop along a similar path together and create a future of mutual co-prosperity and peace?"

To explain the fundamentals of these principles, I have used a verse from the first chapter of the Bible. Genesis 1:28 reveals the following: Then God blessed them, and God said to them, *"Be fruitful and multiply; fill the earth and subdue it; have dominion over the fish of the sea, over the birds of the air, and over every living thing that moves on the earth."*

My interpretation of this verse is that God has given us three primary channels through which we can bring blessings into our lives.

- **The first blessing: Be fruitful.** Become mature, grow and develop, become someone other people would like to enjoy, and prepare yourself so that you can bear healthy seeds that will create the next generation. Do this, and, more than likely, you will sense that your life is full of blessings.
- **The second blessing: Multiply.** Bond with someone of the opposite sex and create a loving family that is capable of multiplication. Do this, and you will, more than likely, gain the feeling of being blessed. And then multiply these blessings by sharing them out into your extended family, your friendships, and your community.
- **The third blessing: Dominion over the creation.** Learn a skill, gain mastery over your physical body, or learn to use money—which represents all things—to generate something meaningful, true, or useful. Learn these things so you can look after the material needs of yourself and your loved ones. Also, make sure you seek to take care of the creation for future generations to enjoy. Do this, and you will, more than likely, gain a feeling of being blessed.

It is noticeable that the core of the three-blessings framework contains no political dimension. God's advice is purely about personal responsibility. "If you, my children, strive to become the best you can be, if you build nurturing marital-families, and if you wisely steward and manage the physical world for the sake of your economic well-being, then, blessings will come. The blessings you receive will be directly connected to your ability to flourish in these three areas of life."

Therefore, in this book, I was asked to explore the deeper layers hidden within this three-blessings worldview.

My explorations ultimately led me to something that should have been obvious from the start—the knowledge that we are a species. Every other species creates optimal outcomes by following the norms of their species. We humans are no different. We achieve the best results for our communities when we live by the species norms that our Creator gave us.

I owe many people my gratitude. I am grateful to those out there who are still fighting for what they know to be right and true. I could not have written this book without them. I also offer many thanks to all those friends who encouraged and helped me in this writing process. They know who they are.

Lastly, I am also deeply indebted to my wife. It is only because of her ongoing support that I could find the time to reflect and learn to see the world in a new way. It is also because she has been willing to stick with me—for better, for worse, for richer, for poorer—that I could become conscious of the deeper core values that we have built our marriage upon. Let our journey begin.

1. ARE WE POLAR BEARS OR PUFFINS?

Are We Polar Bears Or Puffins?

There is a fundamental question that we still are not sure about. "Who are we?"

Every species on earth knows who they are and how their species survives and flourishes. Almost all have been getting on with their lives—dealing with and overcoming challenges—for millions of years. Each species knows its way—its route to well-being and its path to longevity.

The crucial factor that determines whether any species survives for thousands of generations has to do with the offspring they produce. Can enough offspring survive? How healthy and fit are they? If the parent or parents do their job well, then the offspring will grow up and play their role in continuing their own kind.

What about us? We rush through history. We have wars over ideas about who we are. We fill libraries full of books that debate our place within the universe. The cows chew the cud, swish their tails, and wonder how on earth humans can ever survive because they seem so very lost.

But underneath it all, just like all other species, we need to clarify how we bring about optimal outcomes for our children. If we cannot create nations and cultures that ensure the next generation is emotionally, intellectually, and physically healthy, then our cultures or countries will decline. All species depend on the quality of the children that they raise. We are no different.

The family structure that we raise our children in is the one factor that, more than any other, determines whether our children might be morally upright, emotionally whole, and physically healthy.

Every species on earth has one optimal reproductive-cycle, which ensures that they continue through history. Thus, the sea turtle lays hundreds of eggs and hopes one or two survive. Thus, the lions form a pride—a place where one or two males have sexual access to several females—and they all play a part in raising their offspring together. Thus, bald eagles' bond for life and raise several generations of offspring—thereby ensuring the well-being of their species over the long term. In short, we find that each species has one specific method of ensuring that their circle of life continues. No species chooses several different forms of family. There is no reason to select a sub-optimal system of species regeneration when one optimal way exists based on specific environmental factors.

There are several different forms of family structure that a species can choose from to bring about species longevity.

- The single-mother strategy—e.g., bears, reindeer, some spiders
- The matriarchal extended-family—e.g., elephants and bumblebees
- The "lay loads of eggs, walk or swim away, and hope a few survive" strategy—e.g., sea turtles, most types of fish, beetles
- The single-father strategy—e.g., seahorses, some kinds of fish, some toads
- The "one male, several females" harem family structure where a male raises his offspring with his short-term "wives"—e.g., horses, walruses, lions, gorillas
- The "pair bond for a season and raise the offspring together" strategy that most birds use
- The "pair-bond for life and raise all the offspring together" strategy—e.g., love birds, prairie voles, swans, bald eagles, puffins, albatrosses, gibbons, turtle doves, arctic terns, and some penguins

Because we have characteristics much like many other animals, we must ask ourselves some questions. "Which type of family structure has assured the best outcomes for our children and our communities for hundreds of generations? Also, do we see any correlation between the different types of family structures shown above?"

At the start of the twentieth century, every major culture and most minor cultures were marital-family cultures. China, India, Europe, the U.S., the Middle East—all of them were marriage-valuing cultures. We have never had one that flourished over several hundred years through using cohabitation or single parenting. All the evidence points to "opposite-sex pair-bonding for life" being our method of creating unparalleled outcomes for our children, thereby ensuring our nations were sustainable.

When we look at almost all tribal societies that still exist, we find that the only institution that usually does exist in them is the marital family. As a result of the well-being that the marital-family structure offered the community, that tribe may have existed for hundreds if not thousands of generations.

And throughout history, when we look at both tribal societies and nation-states, we find two main types of marital family—the monogamous and the polygamous. But which is our natural form of family structure? Which one ultimately brings about optimal outcomes for our children and our communities? We can only have one, best-outcome family structure—not two.

In the following chapters, I will make the case that, like the puffins and swans, monogamous "pair-bonding for life" is our optimal norm.

The Marital Norms Of The Truelove Species

Many of us have come to believe that men and women are attracted to each other solely for the sake of personal fulfillment—that marriage is primarily about the attraction between adults. Does science support this viewpoint? From a biological perspective, in all animal species that bond for a season or for life, the sexual attraction between the male and female, and the bonding that follows, serves a specific purpose. It serves the well-being and sustainability of their species. Storks do a beautiful heartfelt dance when they reunite every year at the nest and then go on to raise their chicks together. For albatrosses, their joy at their reunion is so intense they make shrill squawks and clash their beaks together, but then they mate and work hard to feed the resultant offspring. Their sense of attraction and life-long "marital" union serves a clear purpose that is far larger than the chemistry between themselves. The magnetism and the partnering that follows exist to serve their offspring's needs and the long-term welfare of their species.

Therefore, marriage has been primarily linked to adults taking responsibility for their biological children. Attraction led to sex. Sex led to children. Their marital promise to each other created an environment that directed their sexual energy towards parenthood. Marriage allowed the couple to fulfill the child's right to protection and, on average, offered them the best possible start to life. Children have complex needs, and take time to grow to maturity. Thus, there is a need for long-term pair-bonding. The turtles just lay eggs and walk away. For humans to have the best chance of surviving, a life-long commitment between parents is needed.

Because marriage primarily concerns the protection and nurturing of the child, then, throughout history, marriage has embodied various internal, child-protecting norms. All truelove species embrace almost all the following behaviors.

The Promise of Fidelity

Most species do not bond for life, or even for a single season. In many, the female typically has to accept the advances of the strongest male. There is no bonding ritual and no long-term union. Thus, there is no concept of fidelity—of being sexually faithful to one partner. Many females have a new sexual partner during each breeding season.

However, when a species does have "marriage for life" as its norm, we also see a strong demand for sexual monogamy. It makes sense. Why make a life-long commitment if your female partner is highly likely to have another male's offspring? And vice versa. If partners were sexually unreliable, why even go through all the effort of seeking to bond? In the animal world, if you want the positives that do come with pair-bonding for life, then you also adopt fidelity. One does not work without the other.

Since humans have a historical strong tendency towards marrying for life, the promise of fidelity has also been part of our social reality. Somewhere in the past, the pledge of sexual loyalty became an integral part of getting married and staying married. This is true for almost every marital-family culture that has ever existed.

Moreover, some scientists today make the case that we, as humans, could only build advanced societies because of fidelity. They note that sexual diseases have been around for a long time. In an age before antibiotics, widespread infidelity would have led to epidemic levels of STDs. The viruses would have eradicated our communities. We are only here today because the expectation of fidelity in marriage became an integral part of our marital norm.

And Affection

Along with fidelity, the ability to sustain a long-term sense of attraction in our marriages also points to the fact that pair-bonding for life is our species norm.

In many species, both males and females have multiple sexual partners across their lives. Alternatively, many females raise their young alone, or the young raise themselves. Because of these methods of reproduction, most species do not develop robust ways of showing enduring male-female affection.

However, almost all species that do make life-long commitments also develop habits that create moments of rich emotional togetherness as a way of sustaining their long relationship. One can call these species "truelove species." Different chemistry is at work.

If, for example, you are a male moose (moose are a single-parent species), then, once a year during the mating season, your testosterone skyrockets. You get a drug-created high for a few days or weeks. You get into some battles, and you maybe get some girls. And then you go back to being your grass-chewing self.

If, however, you are a male albatross, you get a short high when you find the girl of your dreams, you make love a few times, but you also get a warm, ongoing, fuzzy feeling of affection when you are with her. Hormones, such as oxytocin and vasopressin pump through your veins when you see her again after time apart. And dopamine creates feelings of euphoria. As an albatross, you get this joyous emotion for some nine months a year as you raise your child together. Importantly, this ongoing sense of affection is far more enjoyable than the short shot of testosterone-driven lust that comes with sleeping with several females once a year, with very few highs after that. If you like the joy that comes with ongoing affection, you do not want a massive boost of testosterone to keep destroying that. It is one or the other.

Thus, the trueloves sacrifice the opportunity to sleep around. What they get in return is far more valuable—a sense of continuing togetherness and affection.

Humans can instantly connect with the various methods of expressing affection shown by the trueloves. We can enjoy touch and massage (preening), doing things together (e.g., some cranes), snuggling up close (e.g., almost all the trueloves), and dancing together (e.g., some storks). When we express affection in similar ways, we too feel closer to our beloved. As part of the marital deal, humans had to develop—or were given—the capacity to experience a sense of emotional unity which sustains their couple relationships over the long, child-raising years and beyond.

If marriage were not our intrinsic species-norm, we would be unable to sense the beauty of romantic love. If we immersed ourselves in a romantic novel, we would feel no connection and shed no tears. If we want to sustain our marriages, partners need to learn to keep these affection drugs flowing. In doing this, spouses are far less likely to run after other experiences that will trigger other hormones and harm their families.

One can see that many animals that do not bond for life can express fondness and a sense of belonging within their species. Many animal parents show strong bonds of attachment towards their children—touching them, embracing them, being playful with them, and showing deep grief when their children have died. And some express deep emotions towards other pack or group members. Each of these forms of connection serves the needs of each type of family structure—keeping that specific form of family structure durable so that the offspring have the best outcomes.

But here, we are talking about acts of affection and tenderness that keep the relationship healthy because it is the two parents who are seeking to raise the children together—not the pack or the herd or the troupe. Almost all the enduring-love species make sure they regularly express affection to each other. Humans can feel a whole range of bonds of attachment. It is one of the many wonders of being human. But still, our strongest ones are reserved for the parent-child relationship and for the marital partner who will embark on life's journey with us. It is these bonds of attachment that best serve the needs of the child.

In essence, marriage is not just a life-long commitment made between opposite-sex partners. Life-long pair-bonding comes with a package of norms and behaviors. Both fidelity and the potential for strong emotional bonds are part of this package. They both primarily exist as a means to keep the relationship intact to serve child well-being.

Making a Promise Means Something

We do not know when the marital promise came into existence. We have no idea how the first married couple agreed they were married. All we know is that, over time, all major cultures eventually developed a marriage ceremony—a specific moment when individuals from different family backgrounds came to be seen as a new family unit.

Some evolutionary biologists, for example, Dr. Kit Opie, seek to make the case that our development towards becoming who we are today was founded on the development of the marital-family structure. This is because the development of the brain of a human child required many more calories than a single mother could typically find. We see this in tribes that still forage for their livelihood. The women characteristically seek out roots and nuts, or they grow vegetables. The men usually hunt for meat or fish. The marital promise that led to the marital-family structure allowed a mother to increase her daily calorie intake—allowing the fetus to develop a larger brain. This led to the development of the modern human with remarkable brainpower. For those who hold an evolutionist perspective, the marital commitment may well have been the vital step needed to take us from small-brained monkeys that lived in troupes to the highly-intelligent humans we are today.

Historians note that, throughout much of European history, a woman and a man could make a promise to each other—and they were married. They could make this promise on a hilltop, by a river, wherever. The presence of a priest or witnesses was not required for validity. This promise eventually came to be known as the "verbum." If freely given and made in the present tense ("I marry you"), it was unquestionably binding; if made in the future tense ("I will marry you"), it would constitute a betrothal. When people told their neighbors they were married, everyone understood that the male and female were no longer seeking out other sexual partners. The neighbors understood that the couple expected fidelity from each other. Everyone understood that this couple had bonded to protect and nurture their future biological offspring.

In Europe, in 1148, at the Council of Verona, Catholicism made marriage into a sacrament. The church recognized marriage as a place where personal growth took place—a place where a person could grow and mature their spirit into the likeness of Christ. European churches in the Middle Ages also registered marriages, but this was not obligatory. There was typically no State involvement in marriage. It was only some three hundred years ago that lawmakers in Christian nations started regulating marriage within the legal framework.

When we look at modern research on marriage, we find that the marital promise is a vital component of the marital mix. We know from many studies that couple relationships tend to be very fragile without a marital commitment. For example, the vast majority of cohabiting couples with children end up separating before the children reach the age of sixteen—up to 70 percent of them. This compares to a divorce rate of about 20-25 percent for married couples with children. If you want to massively improve your chances of enjoying the benefits of a life-long couple relationship, the marital promise is an integral part of this process.

Research shows us that one of the main reasons for the fragile nature of cohabitation is that the lack of a marital promise profoundly affects the psychological level of commitment, especially where the male is concerned. Males tend to commit to what they do through making a promise, not through moving in together with a partner. Without that promise, a man can always say to himself, "I never promised her anything." Knowing he hasn't promised anything to his girlfriend, he may well give less into their relationship.

More than this, research on children raised by cohabiting parents clearly shows us that they are much more likely to experience an increased number of risks during their childhood. Their parents are more likely to have other sexual partners and are less likely to pool their financial resources to build up family wealth. This often leads to increased levels of poverty. Also, the fear, especially during the tough times that are part of all long-term relationships, that one partner might walk out the door at any time, leads to increased anxiety, more fighting, and higher levels of depression. In summary, because of the natural limits that are inherent in cohabitating relationships, no civilization has ever been built upon them. Too many children, men, and women get hurt, and the communities become too fragile.

Therefore, along with fidelity and the ability to show and feel ongoing acts of affection, the marital-promise is also part of the package that supports our lasting-love norm. The other species that use pair-bonding for life as their norm also have a specific, focused moment where they too unite for life. They might seek to court with several potential partners until they both find a partner with whom they find a natural sense of togetherness. And, at the end of the romantic courtship process, there is a specific moment when both know their commitment to each other is lasting.

In summary, we can say that somewhere in our history, the "pair-bonding for life to bring about the best outcomes for our children" marital-norm became the way our communities continued their journey throughout history. This norm typically contained a marital-promise, fidelity, and ongoing acts of affection. All these elements work together to bring about optimal outcomes for our children. Therefore, marriage is, first and foremost, a child-centered institution, not an adult-centered one. As Ryan Anderson says in his book, *What is Marriage? Man and Woman: A Defense*, "Marriage is a comprehensive, exclusive, permanent union that is intrinsically ordered to producing new life."

Today, many people question this biologically-based, child-focused definition of the word *marriage*—that marriage is first and foremost about creating an optimal environment for children. Some say, "My friends got married and decided not to have children. Does that mean that they are not married?" Alternatively, some people get married in their fifties and thus cannot conceive children together. Are they not married?

The answer is, "Of course, they are married." It is true that many heterosexual married couples today use artificial methods of birth control to prevent themselves from having children, or that some cannot or choose not to have children. However, this does not change the fact that God or Mother Nature gave us pair-bonding for life as our optimal method for raising our young. Notably, the overwhelming majority of these husbands and wives still uphold fidelity. They ensure they don't create children outside of their relationship—children who might face additional risks. Their honorable behavior protects critical social norms.

Bond First, Then Sex

We noted above that all species that bond for life to protect and nurture their offspring have worked out that the successful implementation of their marital-family norm depends heavily on the mutual acceptance of fidelity, a marital promise, and countless moments of positive interaction.

On top of these three elements, there are two other essential norms that need to be followed to ensure the longevity and welfare of all lasting-love species.

- They do not engage in sexual activity until they have chosen each other.
- They very rarely divorce.

For all lasting-love species, there is the norm of no pre-marital sex. In all these species, sexual intercourse only occurs after the partners have chosen each other as life-long partners. Most single-mother species have "one-night stand" sex. Some species create harems, and they have "the toughest guy around" sex. But if you are going to have just one sexual partner in your life, you have to be choosy. You need to sense that this will be a workable partnership. The albatrosses might participate in several years of courtship before they find the right one. The arctic terns fly together high in the sky and play chase, and, when he thinks she is the one, he brings her a fish. During their search for a lasting connection, they do not have any sexual relations.

Why is it so essential that albatrosses, bald eagles, prairie voles, and Atlantic puffins do not engage in pre-marital sex? The answer is pretty simple. Among the truleoves, none of the young have intercourse with a wide range of partners, and then finally decide to settle down with one partner. In the natural world, sex leads to offspring. Those species that practice non-committed sex either have the norm of single-mother parenting, or they lay lots of eggs and walk away, or they raise their offspring in groups. The alternative is that sex only occurs within a committed relationship, one where the male stays around to help raise his children. You cannot have both. There are no "we can sleep around and then bond for life" species. The intricacies of sex do not allow for such species to exist.

So, which are we? What evidence do we have that the norm of limited or no pre-marital sex might also apply to us too, thus showing us more clearly that the standard of enduring-love is how we achieve the best outcomes for our cultures?

Well, if large amounts of uncommitted sexual behavior had been part of our social norm, then communities in the past would have died off because of the rise of STDs. Chlamydia would have made most young women infertile. Beyond this, we see that, throughout human history, there has been a strong desire to limit out-of-wedlock sexual activity. In some cultures, the bride and groom first met on their wedding day. In others, a boy and girl were pledged to each other from birth. Some cultures used matchmakers. In some, people expected that there would be no sexual activity during courtship. However, if sex happened, and the couple created a baby, they got married—even shotgun weddings. Therefore, we see that almost all cultures in history understood that pre-marital sex led to outcomes that weakened their communities. They sought ways to lessen the chance of it happening, and, if it did, the couple would still go down the marital path.

On top of this, one could write a long list of how pre-marital sex harms the lives of people and our societies today. For example, unwanted children, abortions, harmful diseases, the development of a lower sense of commitment, broken hearts, and higher rates of sexual assault all heighten the risk of a more difficult life course. More than this, we find that those couples who do not engage in pre-marital sex have, on average, the most successful marriages we know of. Although many of us are highly resistant to admitting it, the species norm of no pre-marital sex to bring about optimal outcomes for our communities also works for us too.

You and Only You

The last norm that forms part of the package that creates the ability to pair-bond for life is a strong tendency towards life-long monogamy—to no divorce. All the truelove species inherently know that their species stays strong through radically limiting the percentage of couples that separate. For sure, a few of the truelove species do "divorce," and when they do, there is often a bloody battle between two competing males. But, for the sake of the well-being of their offspring, the vast majority of puffins overcome their challenges. Their ability to put up with the difficulties is bolstered by their ability to be affectionate. They snuggle up close and preen each other. For them, this makes their union worthwhile and probably stops divorce from being a more regular occurrence.

Because pair-bonding for life is our species norm, then, across the history of our cultures, we also see a strong tendency towards maintaining our commitment to our marriages, often through thick and thin. Historically, divorce, depending on the culture, was a reasonably rare experience. People lived much shorter lives. Parents understood that they alone were ultimately responsible for their children.

The unique challenge for humans is that expressing the art of affection and offering acts of love are not automatically built into our subconscious or DNA. We somehow know it should be part of our marriages because it is the norm among other lasting-love species. But rather than the art of love and affection occurring instinctively, it seems we all have to make a personal decision to improve our ability to express affectionate love. So, our challenge throughout history has been that we have been given this truelove norm, but, to sustain it, we also have to try to learn the art of loving well.

So, the big question in human history has been, "How can we, as humans, for the sake of the well-being of our offspring, create the kind of culture that supports the growth and learning of marital partners?" This will improve their ability to express ongoing tenderness and warmth towards each other. If we can voluntarily learn to do this, then a hopeful future is ours.

"Mummy And Daddy, Do You Love Me?"

When we look into the data on child well-being, we find something important about being human. We find that children have a deep desire to be loved by both their biological parents. Did we gain this desire through an evolutionary process? Or has this desire been planted in the soul of children by our Creator? Whatever its roots, it is an immensely powerful dynamic that plays a significant role in human well-being.

It is easy to see in the data that somewhere in our development, children developed a strong attachment need, not just to their mother, but to their father too. In troupes of monkeys, the bonding with the mother is vital, but the need for a close connection with the father—whoever he might be—is far less pronounced. In the work of psychologists who study attachment theory today, we can see that a child who has the opportunity to form a reasonably healthy bond with both their biological parents has, on average, a higher chance of building emotionally stable relationships throughout their life. Even in the middle years, the vast majority of us want to know if both our biological parents still love us.

Attachment theory ultimately shows us that we are all born with a deep, innate desire to know the love of both the mother and the father who gave us life. The inner sense that "both my biological parents love me" is a foundational emotion. This knowledge is most likely to keep the child motivated during their school years and keep them out of harm's way. Emotionally secure children are more likely to listen to their parents' requests and to participate in creating an enjoyable family experience. Since the children are already more likely to know they are loved, they are less likely to feel the need to take drugs or overdose on alcohol to numb the feeling of being unloved when they reach adulthood.

The feeling of being emotionally secure is probably the greatest gift we can give to our children. It is the number one predictor of whether the child can grow and create a fulfilling life of their own. Because of this fact, a reasonably healthy emotional bond with both biological parents is the primary dynamic that lays the foundation for family tree and social improvement.

Because the attachment bond plays such an essential role in human well-being, it is often hard for those who have a life experience that breaks the emotional bond with one or both of their parents. Something might happen in a family that causes a child to distrust a parent. Alternatively, they might feel unloved by one parent. As children, we might find it hard to understand that one of our parents had a difficult time as a child, and their adverse experiences are causing them to now act in ways that harm the parent-child bond. As children, we often lack the maturity needed to process a difficult moment with one of our parents—thus allowing forgiveness and reconnection to occur. In response to such events, children can create an attachment trauma. In their hearts, they can build a wall between themselves and one or both of their parents.

For humans, this attachment trauma, this separation from the knowledge that we are loved by the people who gave us life, can sometimes cause havoc with our lives. For example, a married partner often finds that an attachment trauma with one of their parents makes it harder to attach themselves to their spouse. Something their spouse does triggers the hidden pain and anger that is associated with the broken relationship with the parent. What should be something easy to solve becomes overwhelmed by complex and powerful emotions. Then again, some adults today find they have an addiction or struggle with psychological challenges that are linked to their attachment trauma. Today, many adults, even if they were raised in reasonably happy families, seek out professional help as a means to heal their attachment traumas so that they can be freer to live a life that honors their deepest desires. For many adults, the healing of their relationship with their parents is an ongoing theme in their life.

An attachment trauma can occur within any form of family system. However, today, various forms of legislation exist that increase the chances of an attachment trauma being formed.

For example, IVF and surrogacy often create a situation whereby the child will never know the daily love of one of its biological parents. Such children reveal they often feel deep anguish because of this attachment trauma. One only has to visit websites such as anonymousus.org to start to understand their pain. Here is a recently posted poem.

> *You were 23, and in June of that year, you were ready to*
> *receive your Bachelor's degree.*
> *You were in debt, and probably in that moment, the thoughts*
> *of having me weren't what ran through your head.*
> *You jacked off into a bottle for some cash*
> *And just like you tried to forget the life you created, you*

dashed.
But here I am today, wondering what life would've been like if I had a father to this day.
But here I don't stand tall
Struggling without any father, trying not to fall.
You left me before I knew what you were
Do you think if it were up to me, I would've let this occur?
You are the reason I'm here
Thinking of letting my mom know about my knowledge of half-siblings is what hits me with fear.
You are the reason no father will walk me down the aisle
And the fact that I had no say in how I was born is vile.
Now I sit here and hope that you'll claim me as your own
But you've already made a mystery out of any life I've ever known.

And yet again, a hurting young adult wrote the following.

My Moms always made a good image. Smile everybody and pretend to be happy that was our family motto. But I didn't feel happy every time I came home from a friend's house and saw how different it was in their homes. My best friend's dad was the greatest guy he was funny and nice and always taking us places. He listened to us. I was jealous of my friend and wrote the word Daddy on a piece of paper and put it under my pillow. I wanted a Daddy like my friend had. My friend's family all knew how much I liked their Dad cuz I was always asking if I could help him. One day, my friend's mom asks me, "Are you a Daddy's Girl?" It means you are the kind of girl who really loves her Daddy and is real close to him. Well, I went home and cried becuz I don't have that and never will know what that's like...

I am still drawn to older men, fatherly types. Still searching for the Daddy I will never know. You cannot just donate your sperm and walk away because there is so much more to you than a biological contribution. When you walked away, you denied me the chance of ever knowing you

> *and loving you, and you denied yourself the chance to know and love your child. If you donated sperm about 18-20 years ago to two gay women, I could be your daughter. The movie Delivery Man with Vince Vaugh is about a man who meets his sperm donor children as adults. I cried and cried and cried. It was sort of a healing, but it also brought the pain up to the surface again. I know he is out there. I can feel the pull. What am I supposed to do with that?*

And then again, today's divorce laws are not designed to recognize that children need a healthy attachment with both of their biological parents. The legislation instead focuses on the relationship between the adults. When looking at the data, it is evident that divorce increases the child's chances of forming an attachment trauma. What was the emotional pain of the adults might now become the life-long pain of the child.

For example, one would think that if a mother and father divorced, and the mother married again, then the children, with the extra resources that the new stepfather brings into the family, would have the same life outcomes as they would have had in their original family. However, this is not what we find. The children, who now often experience a more complicated relationship with their biological father, are more likely to develop an attachment trauma. Usually, the extra resources can do little to heal this suffering.

Many stepparents act with deep care towards their new stepchildren and end up building loving bonds. But frequently, despite all their hard work, the child puts up barriers or finds it hard to deal with the separation trauma that is often a part of losing the daily affection of their biological father or mother. With such internal turmoil, the child often experiences a more complex future. The researcher Paul Amato found the following.

> *Although the great majority of parents view the formation of a stepfamily positively, children tend to be less enthusiastic. Stepfamily formation is stressful for many*

children because it often involves moving (generally to a different neighborhood or town), adapting to new people in the household, and learning new rules and routines. Moreover, early relationships between stepparents and stepchildren are often tense. Children, especially adolescents, become accustomed to a substantial degree of autonomy in single-parent households. They may resent the monitoring and supervision by stepparents and react with hostility when stepparents attempt to exert authority. Some children experience loyalty conflicts and fear that becoming emotionally close to a stepparent implies betraying the nonresident biological parent. Some become jealous because they must share parental time and attention with the stepparent. And for some children, remarriage ends any lingering hopes that the two biological parents will one day reconcile. Finally, stepchildren are over-represented in official reports of child abuse.

Stepchildren might feel a whole range of negative feelings towards the new stepparent. This is one of the main reasons why stepfamilies have higher levels of divorce. However, the key indicator of positive outcomes for the child in a stepfamily is often not the new stepparent but the enduring bond with their biological parent.

In summary, we can say that children can develop an attachment trauma in any form of family system. However, when the biological parents raise their children together, they automatically have a higher chance of growing up feeling emotionally secure.

This strong desire to know the love of both biological parents reveals why it is impossible to build a flourishing future in a nation that experiences an excessive amount of single parenting. Many single parents do a remarkable job raising their offspring—sometimes even a better job than some two parents do. However, no matter how much they invest in their child, the child's feelings of loss and separation can cause complex emotions that might never be resolved.

The emotional needs of the child clearly show us that the family norm of our species is the marital family. The wedding promise is not just a promise made between adults. It is a promise made by the adults to honor the attachment needs of the child. Children are born expecting that promise to be kept. If single parenting were our species norm, our children would not have such a strong desire in their hearts.

Our Truelove Norm Builds Successful Nations

Looking back in history, the major empires that Europe created all had the same starting point. The great civilizations—the Greek, the Roman, the Teutonic, and the Protestant British—all started from the same foundation. At their inception, they all had the clear expectation of monogamous marriages, of no divorce, of fidelity, and of chastity before marriage—a package of norms named "absolute monogamy." After adopting many of the core elements of our natural species norm, these cultures unleashed a tremendous amount of energy.

Absolute monogamy created the foundation for the rise of democracy and the growth of wealth in ancient Greece. Several centuries later, the Romans copied this marital tradition and placed it into their legislation. The Roman Empire was born. The Teutonic Order of East Europe embedded the same culture of absolute monogamy into their Catholic traditions, and they created a flourishing and prosperous empire from the 1200s onwards. The same happened in the U.K. when the Puritan Protestants came to power in the 1600s. Their norms created the foundation for the British empire—an empire where a tiny island with a population of around ten million people came to make a tremendous impact on world history through spreading democracy, technology, and educational norms. The same marital standards were also at work at the start of both the Sumerian and Babylonian empires, both of which created impressive civilizations that we can see the remnants of today.

Adopting the norms of the trueloves did not always mean that these cultures created marriages abundant in love and affection. The Sumerians seemed to have had the tradition of selling their daughters to the highest bidders as a means of stopping pre-marital sex. But pre-marital sex, infidelity, and divorce were all highly frowned upon. The social stability that these marital laws created caused these cultures to stay energized and focused on cultural development. The energy unleashed allowed for the development of an education system, a growth in prosperity, and the creation of high-quality cultural wealth—libraries, great plays, philosophical thoughts, and more. Great thinkers came to the fore, and astonishing buildings and cities were created.

When the Protestants took control of the British parliament in the 1600s, the culture embodied the norm of absolute monogamy. The process created a higher sense of respect among men, women, and children. This heightened sense of respect translated into a sense of higher being—that people were worthy of a higher standard. An advanced civilization on the pathway towards democratic norms was being born.

In 1934, J.D. Unwin published a book entitled *Sex and Culture*. He made an extensive review of the sexual and family norms of 186 cultures in world history and how these norms related to the flourishing of a nation. He put forward the following findings.

- **The effect of sexual constraints.** Increased sexual restrictions, either pre- or post-nuptial, always led to the increased flourishing of a culture. Conversely, increased sexual freedom invariably led to the collapse of a culture three generations later.
- **The most successful cultures.** Such cultures occurred when both prenuptial chastity and absolute monogamy were present. Rationalist cultures that retained this combination for at least

three generations exceeded all other cultures in every area, including literature, art, science, furniture, architecture, engineering, and agriculture.
- **The single most influential factor.** Surprisingly, the data revealed that the most significant correlation with a culture's success was whether prenuptial chastity was required or not. It had a considerable effect either way.
- **The effect of losing prenuptial chastity.** When prenuptial abstinence was no longer the norm, then absolute monogamy, deism, and rational thinking also disappeared within three generations.
- **Total sexual freedom.** If complete sexual freedom was embraced by a culture, that culture eventually collapsed to the lowest state of flourishing—which Unwin describes as "inert" and at a "dead level of conception." Citizens tend towards selfishness and behaviors that harm their communities. Then, the culture is usually conquered or taken over by another culture with a higher level of social energy.
- **Time lag.** If there is a change in sexual constraints, either increased or decreased restraints, the full effect of that change is not realized until the third generation.

Joseph Unwin wrote the following about his research.

> *No society can display productive social energy unless a new generation inherits a social system under which sexual opportunity is reduced to a minimum. If such a system be preserved, a richer tradition will be created, refined by human entropy.*

Also, in 1976, Sir John Glubb wrote *The Fate of Empires and the Search for Survival*. He reviewed the rise and fall of several civilizations. He noted that civilizations typically lasted for some 250 years and had a similar life-cycle with various stages. He labeled the last step the Age of Decadence, which included materialism, frivolity, an influx of foreigners, the growth of a welfare state, a loss of a sense of civic duty, and the weakening of religion.

One can see this life-cycle in British history—from the Puritans' more puritanical lives to a growing level of sexual adventure in the late Victorian era some three hundred years later. The lack of couple-building skills in many marriages led to increased rates of infidelity and other marriage-harming behaviors. Lawmakers eventually came under pressure to allow for divorces to occur. Furthermore, young adults began to demand that they be freer to choose their partners—believing that this might allow for more loving marriages. But, with this demand, pre-marital sex increased. Today, Britain has high rates of divorce, and each successive generation of young adults finds it harder to get married to best protect their biological children.

The central goal of history then is to reconnect to that which the love birds do so very well. They don't just build pair-bonding unions, but they create affectionate pair-bonding unions, which give them the best chance of sustaining their species. So, we also have the task of creating cultures that value our marital-family norms of minimal pre-marital sex and little divorce, and, additionally, they need to teach each new generation of citizens about the art of loving well. The nations that can develop such families in their communities will have an advantage over all others.

Unlike all nations in the course of history, we live in an era where we have the knowledge needed to build lasting marriages that can express enduring love and affection. Our problem is that our marriage-based Christian culture gave up on waiting for the cavalry to arrive. We started giving up on our marital norms over a hundred years ago. Today, we have many resources to help dating couples and married partners build beautiful marriages, but too few know that this knowledge exists. There is a block somewhere in the system, and most citizens are not receiving the knowledge that they so desperately need to build more meaningful marital families.

In summary, history shows us that the tradition of absolute monogamy can bring about unparalleled levels of energy within a culture. However, it does bring about adverse side effects when couples don't work on their relationships, and affection within their relationship is not consistent. But still, the focusing of the mind of adults on family-tree improvement—on seeking to make sacrifices and achieve personal growth so that your child has the opportunity to build a more secure future than you did—brings about great rewards too. Child well-being is the primary winner. Asking people to stay in complicated marriages is not a death sentence for their culture. But ultimately, if you want people to stay in their marriages, a culture that allows freedom of choice needs to find ways of ensuring that each citizen can improve their ability to express love to their life-long partner.

Marriage Is A Natural Responsibility

It is important to note that heterosexual marriage has nothing to do with legally granted rights. Marriage is primarily about our natural circle of life. The biological parents take responsibility to fulfill the intrinsic wishes of their child. If one has created a new life, one has inherent duties to one's child. When we look at the swans, we see that they do not need a legal right to bond for life.

The heterosexual marital-family is born from the natural needs of children, not out of human thought systems. Marriage existed as the best way to raise and protect our children thousands of years before any political structure was formed. Primarily, it exists for the sake of children who take years to raise. When the children mature, leave home, and marry, their parents serve as a valuable resource. Grandmothers and grandfathers are often at the heart of the extended-family network, keeping the family bonds active and offering valued support along the way. Such has been our circle of life for a long time.

Of course, because of the immense power of our brains, we have dimensions to our lives that the albatrosses and puffins do not exhibit. We, unlike them, are also very social. We like to form group identities, and groups can sometimes create a competitive spirit that does not exist in the world of the arctic terns. The rivalry between sports teams and some companies can often make us look more like pack animals that compete for territory or resources. The social part of ourselves also allows us to form good friendships, something that we might see glimpses of in the lives of other intelligent mammals such as chimpanzees. We also have vast intellectual powers and incredible creativity. We can sense the transcendent, and many feel that they can build a relationship with the divine or a cosmic force. And, we can almost instantly imagine ourselves anywhere in the universe, doing almost anything.

But still, our reproductive process, and the length of time it takes to raise a child, places this part of our lives squarely within the realm of all the other lasting-love species. It is this form of family structure that we see at the base of all human civilizations across history. The better we realize the similarities we have with other enduring-love animals, the faster we will understand how we can build lives and communities that are more in harmony with our natural selves.

In summary, I have to agree with the researcher Ryan Anderson when he writes: -

> *The conjugal view of marriage... has long informed the law—along with the literature, art, philosophy, religion, and social practice—of our civilization. So understood, marriage is a comprehensive union. It unites spouses at all levels of their being—hearts, minds, and bodies, where man and woman form a two-in-one-flesh union. It is based on the anthropological truth that men and women are distinct and complementary, on the biological fact that reproduction requires a man and a woman, and on the sociological reality that children benefit from having a mother and a father. As the act that unites spouses can also create new life, marriage is especially apt for procreation and family life.*

2. SOPHIE AND RICHARD HAVE CHILDREN—A CULTURE IS BORN

Our Marital Norm Creates Cultural Energy

Everything we see in the universe is a manifestation of energy. We eat food to gain energy. We then transform that energy into the creative energy that builds ourselves, our relationships, our businesses, our nations, and our cultures.

To build an atom, you need protons and electrons. Natural laws cause the electrons to spin around the proton as the planets go around the sun. This circular dynamic creates forces that allow the atom to come into existence, sustain itself, and be ready to join up with other atoms to create something new.

The natural world is built from the energy that is generated from the interaction between at least two different entities that work together to create a relationship based on natural laws. For example, a male and female puffin relate with each other based on their inherited norms. Their interaction creates a child, and this new manifestation of energy allows for three positive outcomes for their species.

First, this energy manifests itself in the birth of offspring, which, in turn, forms the basis for the continued existence of their species. Second, the birds' marital-family structure sustains their species' norms. The parents' role-modeling generates energy that helps their offspring learn vital skills that they need to acquire to build their unions and raise their own young.

Thirdly, the puffins' biological union lays the foundation for the possibility of continual development within their family tree. If one of the parents develops the ability to fly a little faster, that ability may be passed down to future generations. All improvements in being, either biological or cultural, might be passed down and, over time, they may spread out across the species. In short, the sexual interaction between the male and female creates forces that trigger a whole chain of constructive events for their species as a whole.

It is the same for us humans. When a male and female bond in a way that aligns with the natural norms of our species, then their union also has the potential to generate social forces that are highly likely to benefit both our present and future communities. The norm of marriage and the creation of biological children generate energy. This energy allows for a culture to continue to exist, sustains its goodness, and provides a platform for its future development. Cultures take generations to build, and our species norm determines that the marital-family structure is one of the central channels through which this long-term progress can occur.

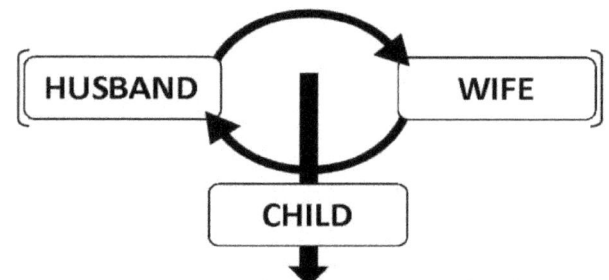

The Social Purpose of Marriage:
The protection and nurturing of the child.
Through the creation of the child, the couple generates forces that allow for the continued existence, sustainability, and development of a culture.

Thus, the marriage of a man and a woman is not just a private affair. Thousands of years ago, raising children under the love and protection of both biological parents became our way of guaranteeing the slow but sure development of our communities.

Step-by-step, we have enjoyed ever-improving life-long outcomes. The affection that the partners feel for each other serves social purposes, not just personal ones.

The Continued Existence Of A Culture

When two married partners, Richard and Sophie, create children, they ensure the continuation of their culture and nation. The Christian-based culture of Europe and the U.S. is probably the most notable culture the world has ever seen. It took generations to build.

However, today, the birth rate in Europe is low. If the birth rate continues its current decline, then Europe will eventually be taken over by people who live by other cultural norms. And maybe that new culture will be unable to replicate many of the marvelous elements that Europe is currently exhibiting. Therefore, we need to have children if we value our culture's ongoing development to ever-higher heights.

Next, when Sophie and Richard hold their newly born child in their arms, this inspires them both to develop a whole host of positive, community-focused attitudes. They are now parents, not individuals. As parents, they are more likely to think about what benefits their child and their community as a whole. Their children push them to develop thoughts such as, "How do we protect this beautiful new life, or raise little Zoe to reach her full potential, or build a safe community for Zoe to venture out into?" They might decide to stop watching violent movies, give up smoking, or begin eating healthier food. They have someone in their life who asks them to move away from selfishness—to move towards more altruistic attitudes and behaviors.

Conversely, in today's Western world, where increasing numbers of adults artificially delay marriage and parenting well into their thirties, or show no desire to have children at all, we see rising levels of me-centered thinking. Thoughts such as "It's my life" or "These are my rights" increase. Such thinking has led to a constant rise in community-harming behaviors among young adults during their twenties, for example, drug abuse and hooking-up. Moreover, this extended-childhood adult lifestyle is causing many challenges for parents who are trying to raise their teenage children. Today, many parents have to worry about protecting their children from pornography, drugs, or early sexual experiences. A lack of a common purpose starts to appear. Cultural decay is the outcome. Thus, throughout history, the existence of children in the vast majority of families created a socially protective mindset that allowed for both social cohesion and cultural longevity. The novelist Peter De Vries made the following insightful comment.

> *The value of marriage is not that adults produce children but that children produce adults.*

And lastly, a child's birth creates a new generation to care for the elderly and the sick. Many people in developed nations like to believe they have left behind the "outdated" concept of having children to provide for them in old age. This is simply an illusion.

In some countries today, there is a birth rate of 1.2 children for each woman. This means that one hundred citizens give birth to sixty citizens, and these sixty citizens will create thirty-six citizens. These thirty-six citizens will have to raise their own children while supporting a much larger group of retired citizens. Also, one runs out of people to do the jobs that need to be done to keep the social fabric moving.

Such a situation leaves governments with two far-from-perfect solutions. One is to place a colossal financial burden on the next generation. The other is to have large-scale immigration of people from a different cultural background. Neither of these options provides for the slow but sure development of one's own culture.

It is crucial for those who live in Western democracies today to understand this fact. Today's democracies took generations of sacrifice to build. It took a long time for people to gain equal rights under the law, for women's rights to be acknowledged, and for the legislation to become color blind. These nations are not perfect because people are not perfect. However, they are a lot better than the corrupt, or authoritarian, or poorly run alternatives that we see all around the world today.

If citizens in these nations lose sight of the goodness that has been achieved and become neglectful of their responsibility within this culture, eventually, the advanced culture they have inherited will be lost. It will not be that their culture just carries on within a smaller population. Their descendants will experience far fewer freedoms and, probably, far more corruption. There is a need to see the good and develop a "missionary zeal" that seeks to offer one's nation as a beacon of hope that people in other countries can aspire to. However, such an example can only be maintained by having enough children.

Thus, if a couple loves their first child, it would be nice to give that child a brother or sister to grow up with and enjoy and help develop their social skills. If a couple cares about their nation, they might have three children to make sure their country stays financially viable. And if a couple values their culture and wants it to expand and grow, they might consider having four children. Noteworthy cultures take time to grow, but you cannot cultivate them if there are not enough children being born.

In summary, when a couple holds their child in their arms, they are doing what no other human relationship can achieve. They are doing the same thing that their parents did, and their grandparents did, and all their ancestors did. They are providing for the continued existence of their culture, giving it time to mature, blossom, and find new, positive solutions to life's challenges.

The Marital Family Sustains A Culture

Ideally, Richard and Sophie, in their interaction with their children, Zoe and Tom, create forces that sustain their healthy cultural norms.

Imagine the Mid-West of America back in 1850. If Sophie and Richard had been around at that time, they might well have been one of the many pioneering families who created a farm. What might their children have learned from them?

- Many of the skills needed to run a home—e.g., cooking, fixing, cleaning, washing, shopping.
- The farming skills needed to feed their own families.
- The development of hobbies—e.g., hunting, fishing, sewing, knitting, painting.
- In going to church every Sunday, the children would have learned how to celebrate the rhythms of life—Christmas, New Year, Easter, Thanksgiving, weddings, funerals, parties, and visiting neighbors. Also, they would have listened to sermons that asked them to improve themselves for the sake of self-development and community well-being.
- Many of the respectful relationship skills that their parents might have exhibited—forgiveness, the gift of serving, the art of being grateful, humor, playfulness, teamwork, core values, nurturing, disciplining, and more. In other words, their family would have been their primary school of love.
- Because Sophie and Richard contributed to the funding of their children's school, the local church, the sheriff, and other community-enhancing institutions, Tom and Zoe would have learned how communities are financially built and sustained.
- Tom would have learned almost everything he would know about being a father from his father, and Zoe would learn much about being a mother from Sophie. And both of them would have learned something about how men and women can sustain their marriages from the way Richard and Sophie interacted with each other.
- In the first two years of life, the children would have probably been raised mainly by their mother, who might have sung them songs of love and joy. As she looked into their eyes, she might have been subconsciously saying, "You are amazing. You can trust my love. You are always worthy of it. I am so glad you

were born into my world. I see, love, and respect the elements of your father that are in you." Such sentences offered both children a tremendous internal resource that they could continuously call upon throughout their life.

- Later, Richard would have become more involved. He would have probably taught them how to ride a horse and how to play outdoor games. He is much more likely to have encouraged them to take risks. His deeper voice and clear, direct sentences would probably have helped in the disciplining of the children. When the children got older, Richard was probably the parent who made it clear that the children had to be home by a specific time or that they should not get overly involved in sexual interaction when they were too young to know what it meant.

Author Warren Farrell, one of the pre-eminent researchers into the effect of fatherlessness on boys, commented: -

> *Dads tend to build bonds with their sons by, for example, playing games and rough-housing, and then use the resulting bond as leverage for their sons to "get to bed on time" lest there be "no playing tomorrow night." This boundary enforcement teaches boys postponed gratification. Boys with minimal or no father involvement more frequently suffer from an addiction to immediate gratification. For example, with minimal or no father involvement, there is a much greater likelihood of video game addiction, more ADHD, worse grades in every subject, less empathy, less assertiveness (but more aggression), fewer social skills, more alienation and loneliness, more obesity, rudderlessness, anger, drugs, drinking, delinquency, disobedience, depression, and suicide.*

Now, in the same year that Tom was born, imagine the life of a fatherless child. Many of these children ended up working for much of their childhood in workhouses—sleeping with other children in dormitories. They had minimal schooling and worked long hours doing tedious, repetitive jobs. What was it like to celebrate life? What was it like to grow to take care of yourself and build a family? Many of these children ended up being servants. All this was happening while Zoe and Tom were riding free across the open plains, after which they went on to start their own successful families and businesses. They had completely different lives because their parents had married and raised their children together.

In essence, throughout history, marriage has created the most protective place we know of for men, women, and children. It has always been the place where children and women are least likely to experience poverty. Today, on average, married couples are wealthier, less lonely, have improved support networks, enjoy better sex lives, experience less abuse, and are healthier than those who choose other routes through life. Our ancestors created marital homes and shaped family-oriented communities. This stability provided the essential element that allowed for the future development of all other social institutions. We, in developed nations, benefit from these other institutions. Today, there is a need to remind ourselves that we, in the West, live in relatively peaceful countries with an advanced standard of living primarily because of that first stabilizing institution—the heterosexual marital-family.

It is essential to understand this reality and ask what might happen to our cultures if the marital-family norm continues its current decline. Who will discipline the children? Where will children learn the art of loving well and respect?

However, the modern feminist may point to Sophie and argue that marriage is sometimes an oppressive place for a woman. It is strange to see such a word used to describe the natural circle of life that has the potential to give rise to so much joy, meaning, and social good. For sure, Sophie had to work hard to raise her children. Housework can overwhelm many married women with children. But it also needs to be pointed out that if Sophie were an unmarried mother with two children, she would have to do everything by herself. Her parental status would "oppress" her far more. By being with Richard, they split some of the chores between them, and laughter and tenderness are always possible. Also, an unmarried Sophie is at a higher risk of experiencing abuse from her visiting boyfriends and is more likely to suffer from depression, loneliness, or poverty.

The ideal pathway forward then is to ask how to improve Sophie's marital experience, not to throw it away. Left alone with their children, millions of women face more challenging lives. One doesn't discard a nice car just because the tires need fixing.

Due to today's cultural noise, we need to ask some questions. "Is it oppression that women experience when they make sacrifices to build a successful family home? Or is it just that volunteering to participate in something as magnificent as the creation and raising of new life inherently entails meaningful sacrifice?" And also, "Is it solely the women who have to make sacrifices?" Many men work in menial, labor-intensive jobs, or dangerous jobs, all for the sake of love. Many would say that it is impossible to experience love without giving. Also, "Where is a woman most likely to feel she is living a meaningful life—one that inspires her to find joy and feel that she has made a positive contribution to this world?" Is she meant to find the most profound meaning in life, and her most joyous moments, working as a liberated single woman in a factory, driving a bus, or working in a shop? For sure, such jobs can be meaningful. But is work the only place where we can find meaning or even the place where we find the most meaning? On her death bed, is a woman more likely to regret that she didn't spend enough time working in her office or factory or regret that she didn't have enough time to build something beautiful with her children and grandchildren?

In seeking to understand how vital the marital family is to social and cultural well-being, one might also look at how the total number of different religions has reduced over time. There once were hundreds of faiths. Now, there is a concentration of some five to six major faiths. Almost all the religions that lasted encouraged marital-family norms. By supporting and encouraging citizens in their matrimonial duties, these religions gained a competitive edge over other faiths that might have focused on different aspects of our human identity.

In summary, we can say that the marital home is the natural school of love. It is the principal place where children are most likely to learn about respect and the art of loving and living well. It is also where children are most likely to develop their social skills and come to understand social norms. All these qualities allow the children to move forward with their lives. As children inherit the good of the past, this provides for cultural longevity. Thus, the marital family plays a vital role in laying a foundation for long-term cultural stability. Therefore, a researcher, Theodora Ooms, once wrote: -

> Society should try to help more children grow up with their biological, married parents in a reasonably healthy, stable relationship—not to pay respect to a Victorian idea of proper behavior, but because the overwhelming consensus of research shows that's the very best way to raise children.

The Marital Family And Cultural Development

Lastly, the marital family lays the foundation for the future development of their culture through the process of lineage improvement. If either Sophie or Richard develops some new skills, this development might get passed onto Zoe and Tom, thus allowing their children to live a more enriched life. Over time, these small developments might be passed on down the family tree, allowing for the descendants to benefit too. Also, these developments might be transferred out into the wider community. It is the improvement in the wholesomeness of the next generation of citizens that is the fundamental root cause behind all long-term social development.

When we enter a relationship with any human being, then a natural demand for personal growth is bound to appear. In a marriage, a sports team, a company department, a friendship, or in our relationships with our children, tensions are bound to arise. The strains are just a signal that some form of growth or healing needs to take place for harmony and cooperation to reappear. This call for development or healing can take place on any one of three levels.

The first level of growth sees each type of relationship as having certain elements that need to be encouraged for that relationship to work. There are fundamental things that need to take place to keep a company department running (e.g., well-designed job descriptions, a workable complaints procedure, a schedule, etc.). There are also essential behaviors that are intrinsic to the building of a family or the raising of children (e.g., enjoyable mealtimes and managing finances). Neglecting these critical issues just causes stress. When partners work on solving the fundamentals, outcomes can sometimes rapidly improve.

The second level looks at what an individual might improve within him- or herself so that the relationship might develop, thus leading to healthier outcomes. A boss can take self-development courses, and, due to an improvement in his listening skills, workers come to feel empowered. If a teacher can cultivate better disciplining skills, student behavior might start to improve.

The third level looks at the past traumas that seek to disrupt the smooth flowing of today's relationship. For example, if, a few years ago, a thoughtless boss randomly fired many workers in an underhand way, today's employees are less likely to care about the company because they know it doesn't honestly care about them. Then, when the firm hires a new boss, he is clueless about why the employees lack energy. A healing process can start to happen when the company begins to acknowledge these hidden traumas.

One can look at the development of marriage education courses and books over the last fifty years. The first wave of materials primarily focused on marriage as a "project" that the couple needed to work on together. Married partners benefit from spending time enjoying each other's company, or they need to regularly talk about their money issues, children, or the roles they are expecting each other to take. Alternatively, the materials sought to help men better understand women, and women better understand men (e.g., *Men Are from Mars, Women Are from Venus*).

The second wave of materials like *The 7 Principles of Making Marriage Work* and *The 5 Love Languages* helped the individual partners think about how they might improve their various competencies, core values, or attitudes to elicit a potentially improved response from their partner. For example, if a wife learned to focus more on the good that her husband was doing and sent him positive feedback, might this inspire him to give more into the relationship?

Alternatively, he might take responsibility to do a few more of the small, urgent jobs that needed to be done throughout the day. If he lay the table, made the bed, took a few minutes to read to the children—might she feel less stress and respond to him more positively?

The third wave of materials started to focus on helping the partners understand each other's traumas. In revealing this hidden pain, shame, anger, or fear, partners became more aware of how past events harmed their existing relationship. In this new level of awareness, they could often focus on improving their behaviors. Understanding each other's traumas created more patience, compassion, and forgiveness between them. Thus, we have, for example, Sue Johnson's book, *Hold Me Tight*—a book that has been clinically proven to help couples work through many of their most challenging issues.

The growth and healing that two individuals bound by marriage go through play an incredibly important role in the development of societies and cultures. Today's couples need to see that millions of others have evolved to end their difficulties, and they can too. If it were easy to walk away, much of this growth would never take place. As marriage educator Harville Hendrix so clearly expressed: -

> *Marriage is not a static state between two unchanging people. Marriage is a psychological and spiritual journey that begins in the ecstasy of attraction, meanders through a rocky stretch of self-discovery, and culminates in the creation of an intimate, joyful, lifelong union.*

Marriage is not like a car or computer. With a car, we don't need to know mechanics to drive one. We can let someone else repair it when it goes wrong. However, in our marriages, we all need to have a considerable amount of knowledge to know how to deal with the many problems that do arise. Falling in love is maybe the easiest part. Knowing how to maintain that feeling, or how to get it back when it disappears, is a different story. We would all benefit from having a wide range of background knowledge that we can call upon when various new problems arise. Most of us have some knowledge of mathematics, and we use this knowledge daily to improve the quality of our lives. However, most of us have never read a book on marriage enrichment or communication skills. Many of us just use the skills we have gained through osmosis, and we use them repeatedly, even if they do not work. That's what happens when knowledge is lacking.

Thus, married partners rely on their strengths but also need to develop their potential. There is no way around this issue. The education system, the companies we work for, the media, our extended family, books, a faith community, counseling, friendships, sports clubs, a stimulating hobby, life coaching, and attending marriage preparation and enrichment seminars can all offer developmental resources. With the parents gaining all this extra support, the children have a better chance of growing up to have a more enriched life than their parents. Those cultures that find the best ways to support lineage development within the marital families of their citizens, over time, grow to be the healthiest and most successful.

Thus, marriage is a place where partners are bound together on a path of growth. The psychologist and lecturer, Dr. Jordan Peterson, sees the absolute need for struggles that lead to development within a couple relationship. Thus, he remarked: -

> *You want to tangle your life together with someone. It's like two ropes that are tangled together. You are both stronger in times of difficulty, and you have two brains, which is useful when life is complicated...*
>
> *I think you can see the marriage relationship like wrestling. People think of marriage as living happily-ever-after. That's not what you want in a marriage. You want someone to contend with. You learn through that wrestling. You learn where you're an idiot, and where you should stop being one, and vice versa. That's the spiritual aspect of marriage. The fact that you have to contend with someone under all sorts of circumstances is a matter of promoting psychological or spiritual growth, and it's genuine. That's why marriage is seen to be a sacrament in most human communities. It's not just a physiological union. I do think it's dreadful not to have that.*

It is the process of lineage improvement that has been at the core of our development from struggling, prehistoric, tribal communities to today's advanced societies. We understand inter-generational advancement in other areas of human endeavors. This generation of ice-skaters has learned from the technical skills of the previous generations. As humans, we tend to take the level of abilities that our parents could offer, and, ideally, we seek to improve these skills for the benefit of our children and the wider society.

Lineage improvement might be defined as, "Adults, at the age of twenty, with the large investment by their parents, extended family, and society, have a greater ability than their parents did at the age of twenty to build and sustain their own marital family. They also have more skills to offer their children and society than their parents did." When looking at their twenty-year-old child, if parents can say, "In a range of ways, our child is a better human being than we were," then they can feel a deep sense of pride. It is a job well done. They know that their investment and the support systems they have found along their parenting journey have made the world a better place.

There are many ways in which children might experience lineage improvement.

- An increased ability to create wealth within their family system
- A higher level of academic achievement or technical skills
- Improved relationship skills
- Improved emotional well-being and lower rates of addiction
- Fewer behavioral problems
- An improved moral character
- Lower rates of traumatization through sexual or physical abuse
- An increased ability to build a lasting marital-family of their own

When lineage development occurs within the family system, the young generation can offer their improved skills to the wider world through their work or community activities.

However, just as lineage improvement can take place, so can lineage decline. A parent, when looking at their child, can say to him- or herself, "In a range of ways, my twenty-year-old child appears to be less able to build and sustain a marital family than I was."

A range of processes can lead to a higher chance of lineage decline, but four primary possibilities exist.

- Widespread social distress—wars, famine, and financial collapse— can massively weaken a child's outcomes.

- Social support systems in a culture can weaken from one generation to the next. When this happens, there is less overall support for the child's development. For example, poor political leadership can lead to declining educational outcomes. Or an injurious political system such as an authoritarian dictatorship can cause massive harm. Or various elements of a culture can seek to undermine supportive religious communities. And yet again, a culture can start telling lies to its children. Today, our culture falsely tells young adults that marriage and fragile cohabitation are one and the same. This lie will bring harm to many adults' lives and their nations.
- The children themselves can make poor life choices. For example, addictions and laziness can harm their personal growth.
- Lastly, a child can experience less support from their biological parents and extended family than their parents did.

Therefore, it is essential to examine some of the fundamental laws at work within the process of lineage improvement.

First, poor political leadership can harm the social fabric and cause a culture to underperform. However, if the marital-family norm is reasonably intact, then that culture can still survive for hundreds of years. The same is not true in reverse. The "pair-bonding for life to gain the best outcomes for our biological children" family structure is so essential for cultural well-being that a nation that abandons it will go into decline. History teaches us that if too many children experience lineage decline, cultures can quickly disappear and be taken over by their more marriage-valuing neighbors. Today, we witness the Western world leaving behind their marital-family norm, and a large amount of lineage decline is occurring. Many of today's young adults find that they are less equipped for life than their parents were.

In 2016, Robert Putnam authored *Our Kids: The American Dream in Crisis.* He made an insightful analysis of the roots of the current social ills in America. He noted how the present-day breakdown of family structures, parenting, and communities has led to a situation where many teenagers grow up completely unable to move forward with their lives. He commented on how, when he was a child, no matter which racial group or economic background you came from, almost everyone grew up to have a better quality of life than their parents (about 90 percent). He realized that this is not the case for many young citizens anymore (about 50 percent). The support system of both parents, both sets of grandparents, and a church community has now disappeared for many children. He also added to this list the brokenness of the public-school system. Many would agree that a substantial number of schools in the U.S. are now primarily designed to look after the needs of adults—of teachers—rather than children.

Robert found that today, without all these supportive community structures, many young children fall behind in various areas of development. It is almost impossible for a lot of these children to overcome their challenging start in life. Many have suffered lineage decline. Lineage deterioration is happening on a large scale among certain groups within the American population.

Of course, lineage decay can happen within intact marital-families too. Tom might hang out with the wrong teens and get caught up in all kinds of damaging behaviors. Lineage decay may occur in 10-15 percent of marital families. But society can handle this amount of damage because, in the vast majority of other marriages, lineage improvement is still occurring. On the other hand, when we raise our children outside of the traditional family, the rate of lineage decay increases substantially. Of course, many single parents do a remarkable job in what can sometimes be quite challenging circumstances. Many of their children grow up to be as well-rounded as children raised by their two biological parents. This is especially true if the biological father maintains a healthy connection with them. Many of these children grow into adult citizens who are determined to make a positive contribution to the world, even despite their more challenging start in life.

However, it is just a reality that many children raised in a single-parent home face additional risk. Less money, no father to discipline them, demotivation, the development of an attachment trauma, and other issues can all take their toll on the child's development. This being so, maybe 25-35 percent of children might end up having fewer abilities than their parents. Furthermore, some of the harm such children experience is acutely traumatizing. Such occurrences have the potential to have a profoundly negative effect on their entire life. Because of these additional risks, many of them grow up and then find it hard to participate fully in life. They might frequently end up in jail, become addicted, have anger management issues, and much more. With increased levels of lineage decay occurring, cultural deterioration also comes about.

The second fundamental dynamic at work within the process of lineage improvement is the core idea that the quality of the parents/child relationship is the most important relationship when it comes to the sustainability and development of a culture.

When one studies the data on a deeper level, one has to come to a radical and challenging conclusion. The data almost certainly points to the fact that the *only* form of family system that can lay the foundation for continual, family-tree improvement—and constant social progress—is the heterosexual marital–family. Of course, by itself, marriage isn't the only dynamic that brings about the development of cultures. Other elements—like an education system and a judicious level of personal integrity—are needed as well. But without a reasonably successful marital-family norm, it seems like continual development is just impossible.

It seems like humans experience the same boundary that all other animal species experience with their family structure. Both they and we have only one form of family structure that can ensure lasting community well-being. If any animal left its natural family structure, it too would decline. If lionesses tried to raise their cubs alone, or if sea turtles decided they only wanted to lay three eggs, or if chickens chose to bury their eggs under the sand as the sea turtles do, then one would have little hope for the continuation of their species. For humans, the marital family is our way forward. All other methods of raising children seem to have, on average, inherent weaknesses which often create additional risks and lineage decline.

Due to this fact, today, we see two main problems affecting almost every developed nation that has moved away from our marital-family norm.

Firstly, as we raise ever-growing numbers of children outside of the marital-family norm, growing numbers of people struggle on the edge of society. Homelessness, loneliness, mental health issues, and addictions all rise. Sadly, this number grows by the year. While some groups enjoy the full benefits of the modern era, others are experiencing a lower quality of life than their parents.

Secondly, family distress causes immense financial costs for those developed nations with a Christian heritage. After forty years of high rates of divorce, separation, and single parenting, most of these nations are now heavily in debt. In the past, lineage decline led to the extinction of a country or culture. In today's world, we have political systems that seem willing to place an enormous debt burden on citizens who are yet to be born. Prisons, social workers, courts, police, drug rehabilitation centers, welfare payments where there is only a single parent in the home, and many other costs are all extra expenses linked to lineage decline.

In summary, the daily learning that takes place within a marital-family home provides society with some of the foundational energy upon which a civilization builds future development. No other form of human relationship can offer the same basis for both lineage and social improvement across generations. It is the ability to take the present level of goodness, and then improve on this in the next generation, that makes the marital-family structure an institution of supreme importance. No other form of human relationship can achieve this feat to the depth and level that the marital family can.

Of course, all these blessings depend upon the fulfillment of human responsibility. How much do the husband and wife, for the sake of the social good, invest in their marital relationship and into their relationship with their children? Societies can sometimes rise and fall based on the level of this investment.

As we can see, the marital-family structure that humans can enjoy plays the same role as it does among all other lasting-love species. The life-long bond of the couple and the creation and protection of children generate energy that supports the continued existence, sustainability, and development of a nation and culture.

3. THE THREE-BLESSINGS FRAMEWORK

The Three Ways That Humans Receive Blessings

My theory is that our optimal family structure has parallels with the family structure that some other species use to protect the well-being of their offspring. The history of successful civilizations, our love stories, our romantic music, and the data on child well-being all confirm this reality. We are a truelove species, but we have hitherto failed to develop the cultures that can continually live up to this standard. If we look at other features that all these truelove animals exhibit, we might learn some useful things about our human societies that can help us improve.

There are three forms of being that allow for all lasting-love species to thrive.

- **The individual growth drive.** This first dynamic is the individual's natural impulse to strive to be a healthy, mature member of their species. The young African penguin learns to swim, fish, and take care of itself. Its primary goal is to grow to become a reasonably acceptable representative of an African penguin.
- **Successful bonding and parenting skills.** Next, the young puffin has to raise itself to a level where it can show its potential mate that it has some of the core skills and attitudes which play a valuable role in building a lasting partnership. In all lasting-love species, the male doesn't have to fight other males for the right to pair-bond with the female. They have to convince each other that they are both ready for the task ahead.
- **Family economics**. Lastly, the parents need to find enough food to maintain their health and the physical well-being of

their young. Sometimes, it is the male who has to bring home the "pay packet" for the family, for example, the male bald eagle. In some other lasting-love species, both the male and female catch food. They also have to ensure that they do not create scenarios where they cause irreversible degradation to their environment—thus harming future generations of their species.

When almost all individuals in any truelove species do these three things to a reasonable level of competence, then their species is offered ongoing success. The well-being of each pair-bonding species is built primarily upon the health and well-being of countless individuals who are striving to prepare themselves to be successful partners in family building. There's a circle-of-life effect where good parenting produces healthy children who are more likely to aspire to become virtuous partners and parents.

If there is a strong correlation between the human life-cycle and other lasting-love species, we would also expect to see all these three dynamics playing a vital role in human cultural well-being. Suppose most of us aspire to become reasonably wholesome examples of being human, and we best prepare ourselves for the marital-family journey. Would our societies be all the healthier because of this effort? The answer is evidently, "Yes." Also, when a husband or wife, or both, strive to learn the necessary skills to feed their family, are our communities, on average, healthier places? Again, we can answer in the affirmative.

Moreover, these areas of responsibility seem to align with those things that appear to bring us the most meaning in our lives. If we pursue them, all of these responsibilities can offer us a deep sense of meaningful engagement or joy. We see this in the field of positive psychology today. Research shows that people find their greatest joy in three primary places. We can get good at something—art, dance, chess, cooking—and as we do so, our level of joy probably increases. Psychologists call this "flow." We also can find great joy in our families and friendships. Lastly, we tend to enjoy having a challenging profession that is socially meaningful.

These three primary sources of happiness correlate with our three primary human responsibilities. As we move forward with any of these, we automatically receive positive feedback in the form of joy and a sense of personal meaning. If we do not have worthy goals to strive towards, we often tend to look for enjoyment in impulsive pleasures. These spontaneous pleasures often don't bring about constructive, medium- to long-term outcomes for individuals or communities.

It's useful to look more deeply at the dynamics of personal growth, family building, and our work ethic within the context of being human.

1) The "Reasonably Mature" Individual

We don't have a word in the English language that describes the attributes of a reasonably developed young adult who would make for a wholesome partner in marriage and a reasonable parent. We have phrases such as "a man or woman of character" and a "wholehearted individual," but these only represent some aspects of a well-rounded, mature, young adult. Below are some of the characteristics that a thoughtful, wholesome, young adult might possess.

- Reasonable intellectual development
- Integrity based on timeless core values (e.g., don't murder, steal, or lie), including respectful use of one's sexual nature
- We might include a desire to keep physically fit
- Relationally competent—I can solve conflicts with my friends or work colleagues, understand fairness, have empathy and the ability to say sorry, etc.
- Develop essential life skills. Be on time, dress appropriately, make goals and keep them, etc.

- She or he understands the attitudes that lead us towards personal growth and an inner sense of well-being. From a positive psychology perspective, these attitudes might include seeking to be grateful and appreciative, trying to find opportunities for growth during challenging moments, the ability to forgive, and a desire to learn and grow through seeking to make a positive contribution in all one's endeavors.
- Human wholesomeness also includes a desire to work on and heal any trauma-based behaviors or thinking patterns. We all, in one way or another, lose the innocent nature we were born with. It gets chipped or broken somewhere in our childhood. This emotional damage can sometimes cause us to act or speak in ways that might harm ourselves or others. In general, it's good to seek to lessen the adverse effects of these trauma-based behaviors by trying to heal.

Who you have decided to be—in terms of your overall attitudes, core values, and behaviors—plays an essential role in your marriage, parenting, work, and friendships. If we get this somewhat right, society will then benefit from the quality of our wholesomeness. In his counseling work, Dr. Jordan Peterson sees how personal growth is a natural outcome of the Christian mindset. He observed: -

> *If you look at the top of the dome of a medieval cathedral, you will see an image of Christ. Think of that picture as representing the ideal individual. That's what you are aiming at, the perfection of yourself, and such a goal will keep you busy for your entire life. Such a goal will do no harm. It will make you better and make your family and community better.*
>
> *Such a goal is psychologically meaningful. By strengthening yourself, you are better able to withstand suffering and overcome malevolence. If you become a better person, then you start to become good for things. You can fix problems and be better able to handle complex situations. It is psychologically meaningful to pursue the highest goals*

and develop your character. It is also the best thing you can do, right here and now, to make the world less terrible than it might be.*

2) Family Relationships

How can I become a person who can choose a compatible life-long partner? How can I also invest in my marital relationship and my children so that my family ends up having a positive influence on our community? What skills do I need to develop, allowing us to become a successful, loving team?

Also, how does our family contribute to our community? Maybe through our faith community, or volunteerism, or by creating a caring neighborhood spirit—one that crosses over racial or religious divides. We all might have our calling. For those who are having a difficult time in life, for those in need of help, a variety of sources of support ideally exist—extended family, friends, a faith community, local charities, and State help are all part of the mix.

3) Economic Self-Sufficiency

I seek to enrich my community through my work. If possible, I aim to bring home a pay packet or develop a business so our family is self-sufficient. I serve my customers honorably and to the best of my ability, and also seek to take care of the environment for future generations. My ability to fulfill my responsibility to my family is most likely to happen in a free market economy. Also, a properly regulated free market is most likely to create a moral society. Why? Because it creates a potent positive feedback loop. We do not like to do business with people who mistreat us or abuse our trust.

If most of us could live the core rules that apply to all lasting-love species, then the result would be maturing communities. Thus, writers for the Royal Society wrote: -

> *It is worth speculating that the spread of normative monogamy, which represents a form of egalitarianism, may*

have helped create the conditions for the emergence of democracy and political equality at all levels of government. Within the anthropological record, there is a statistical linkage between democratic institutions and normative monogamy. Pushing this point, these authors argue that dissipating the pool of unmarried males weakens despots, as it reduces their ability to find soldiers or henchmen. Reduced crime (because most men were married) would also weaken despots' claims to be all that stands between ordinary citizens and chaos. Historically, we know that universal monogamous marriage preceded the emergence of democratic institutions in Europe and the rise of notions of equality between the sexes... In the modern world, analyses of cross-national data reveal positive statistical relationships between the strength of normative monogamy with both democratic rights and civil liberties.

The way that all lasting-love species keep their communities healthy is through the process of each individual striving to become as wholesome as possible. They then apply that wholesomeness to their family life and responsibility to feed their family. And the vast majority of us dream that our son or daughter will mature into a caring, reasonably-intelligent adult, that they might find a career they can find happiness in, and that they can build a loving home to raise their children in. These hopes are intrinsic to being human. The way that humans are created shows us that we gain optimal psychological and physical well-being when we can live out a three-blessings lifestyle.

When looking at all truelove species, they have no "top-down" structure to their communities. They are all equal. They individually fulfill their responsibilities, and their species flourish. There is no authoritarian structure wherein some individuals say they have more power than others. Imagine your nation as one large community of albatross nests, with each home representing a nest. Citizens can choose competent representatives to discuss issues that affect all. But these representatives have an equal value to all other citizens and are merely seeking ways to support all albatross families as a community. Thus, democracy is born. And democracies have proven to be powerful drivers of both growth and prosperity.

If it is true that our species norm is similar to the norm of other lasting-love species, then we would have clear evidence in the recent history of humankind.

Let us look back and imagine our married couple—Sophie and Richard—living on a ranch in the Midwest of America back in 1850. They worked to develop their skills so they could run a successful farm to feed their family. Their farming needs drew in tradesfolk—shopkeepers, blacksmiths, funeral parlors, and more. To support their efforts to raise their children, Sophie and Richard, along with other families, would have paid for the building of a church, a school, a sheriff to protect them, and a judge to settle disputes. Christian colleges, funded by generous donations from individuals, trained these judges. There was very little government involvement. For sure, they elected political representatives who ideally supported their hopes and dreams. They also had to pay some taxes, and these taxes paid for the army and little else. The need for a cumbersome government was not there.

And out of the hard work of couples like Sophie and Richard, prosperous cities quickly grew. And people came to America. Most immigrants wanted to participate in a life where they could build marital families in the land of the free. They wanted to experience the freedom of creating their family without the massive intrusion of an oppressive political structure or an overbearing king. And from this freedom, the U.S. rapidly grew to become the most prosperous nation on earth. Therefore, it is evident that we do not need large government structures to build flourishing communities. We need people who have a common understanding of their expected responsibilities, and then their communities will automatically start to gain blessings.

Thus, we come to understand something more about the topic that this book seeks to explore. All the lasting-love species live a three-blessings lifestyle, as mentioned in the Bible. God or Mother Nature has designed us to sense that we are blessed through the act of fulfilling our inherent responsibilities—be fruitful, multiply, and take dominion.

The Inner Workings Of The First And Third Blessing

We saw above that our marital norm brings about the optimal outcomes for the wider society because, in the act of creating and raising biological children, it creates positive social energy.

However, it is not just the second blessing that creates such forces. The first and third blessing are also called blessings because they generate energy that can produce the same positive social forces. When a culture can create an environment where individuals have a reasonable level of wholesomeness, this also allows for a higher chance for positive social outcomes. And when a culture follows the laws that allow for greater economic dynamism and sustainability, the culture will also reap the benefits.

In the first blessing, we create positive social energy when our mind and body interact using the natural principles we live under as a species. This natural interaction between two entities—our mind and our body—allows us to create our lives, and our actions create energy that ripples out and positively affects our communities and cultures. A great sportswoman can uplift a nation, and a talented singer can bring joy to many citizens. An inspiring teacher can help the growth of many a child.

In the third blessing, we create positive social energy when we relate with the natural world according to the inherent economic principles that we live under. This natural interaction between two separate entities—between those skills which we have developed to bring about financial reward and all aspects of the physical world—generates energy that ripples out and affects the wider community. Bill Gates built a computer, Microsoft was born.

Both types of interaction—the give and take between mind and body, and the give and take between my professional skills and the creation—have the potential to create energy that allows for the continued existence, sustainability, and development of a culture.

Furthermore, we previously saw that marriage contains internal workings that aim to protect the child and the wider society. The same applies to the other two blessings. Once again, we can look to the other truelove species to understand these inner workings.

Suppose one considers the environmental factors that allow a puffin or albatross to feed itself and its family. There are probably four key foundation stones that underpin the third blessing. They are: -

1. Not too many predators
2. They get to keep most of the fish that their talents allow them to catch
3. The eco-system is supportive. The environment supports the puffins' desire to catch fish
4. The albatrosses or puffins themselves do not degrade the eco-system to the point that it can no longer support them

For humans, these foundation stones are similar. They are: -

1. The integrity of individuals, the legal system, businesses, and politicians (almost no sharks)
2. Individuals and companies get to keep most of the money their abilities and skills create
3. Politicians and communities endeavor to support the economic environment—roads, laws, education, etc.
4. Do not destroy the eco-system that feeds us

Because these elements are intrinsic to the building of a healthy economic system, the economist and Nobel Prize winner Milton Friedman wrote the following.

> *A government has three primary functions. It should provide for military defense of the nation. It should enforce*

contracts between individuals. It should protect citizens from crimes against themselves or their property. When the government, in pursuit of good intentions, tries to rearrange the economy, legislate morality, or help special interests, the costs come in inefficiency, lack of motivation, and loss of freedom. Government should be a referee, not an active player.

Over the last thirty years, the ex-communist countries of Russia and China have opened themselves up to the free-market trading system. Citizens now get to keep most of what they earn, some legal protections are offered, and the economic environment has been developed. Today, these countries have experienced an economic boom, the like of which has never been seen before. Playing by the rules that Mother Nature has provided for us as a truelove species has allowed for these blessings.

Also, we saw that the social purpose of marriage was to create a place where children were most likely to flourish. The primary purpose of the third blessing is to allow a citizen to feed, house, and clothe themselves and their family.

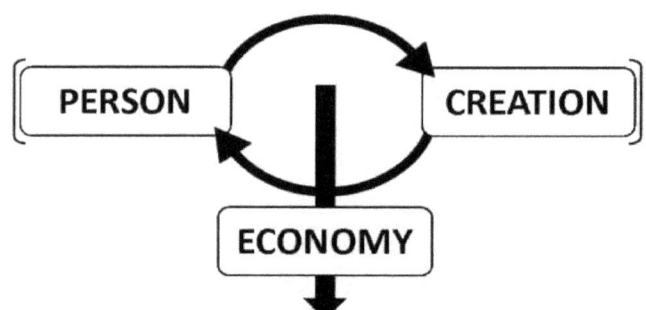

The Social Purpose of Work:
To feed, house, and clothe family.
Through the pursuit of creating a sellable product or service, the individual generates forces that allow for the continued existence, sustainability, and development of a culture.

The Three Blessings Framework

The first blessing—that of personal growth and development—also has to embody various elements that a young adult swan needs to exemplify to be considered a potential life-long partner. These also have parallels with human development.

Both swans and humans need the following.

1. The ability of the new generation to recognize the essential behaviors, core values, traditions, and attitudes that have kept their species resilient in previous generations.
2. The self-development drive—the individual desire to take responsibility to set oneself on a path that leads to ongoing growth and mastery.

The central purpose of my attempt to become a fruitful person is probably something along the lines of, "I left the world a better place than I found it" or "I have improved on the skills that I was given and thus encouraged the process of lineage improvement."

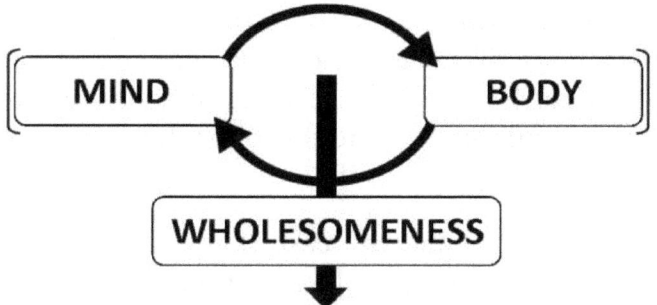

It is upon these essential norms that nations rise and fall. Suppose the young forget valuable traditions and core values, or fail to develop the attitudes that allow them to work on their personal development. In that case, their culture will decline and eventually die.

Luckily, if we strengthen any of the foundation stones that form the core of any of the three blessings, our communities will start to recover. Once one understands the basic rules, it is much easier to see why some nations have seen startling development over the last fifty years and why some countries are still struggling.

All Religions Seek To Uphold Our Species Norms

Over the last four hundred years, Christian-based democracies with a free market system embedded in them have become—based on many different criteria—the most prosperous nations that the world has ever seen. Why might this be the case?

If my theory is correct, Christian-based democracies have been fruitful because the worldview that the Bible gives rise to is in harmony with the three-blessings framework that the trueloves live under. Through encouraging, to some reasonable degree, the three core dynamics that allow for the successful development of all lasting-love species, the Bible taught citizens how to create sustainable communities that could shelter them from the suffering that might happen throughout life.

Atheists often seek to make the case that Christianity is a crutch, that the faithful are leaning on Jesus rather than seeking personal growth. Sometimes this is true. But, on the whole, the exact opposite is much more accurate. The worldview that emanates from the Old and New Testaments encourages personal development and personal responsibility in line with our inherited three-blessings norm. This is the fundamental reason why Western nations have ultimately become so successful. Becoming responsible is the exact opposite of a crutch. We create a sustainable culture when most citizens agree to limit their behavior around a worldview that embodies life-giving forces. Citizens did this because they could see that the life-giving forces were worth more than what they were asked to give up.

The Three Blessings Framework

Let us briefly look at how the Biblical worldview encourages citizens to live a life that embraces the three core dynamics that all truelove species embody.

- The Ten Commandments provide the fundamental core values that citizens are advised to live by to create the foundation for building a thriving community. Community building is almost impossible if people choose to steal from each other, if infidelity is prevalent, or if people murder, lie, and allow jealousy to fill their hearts.
- The Biblical mindset encourages individuals to develop their relationship skills and to have a personal growth orientation to life (e.g., serve others, develop your talents, appreciate the good in others, find the silver lining in difficulties, learn to forgive, etc.).
- Protestantism, especially, drew out the parts of the Bible that encouraged a strong work ethic and integrity in business.
- Christianity helps people understand that we are all in need of healing. Through experiencing the intense love that Jesus has for each person, many Christians have felt free to let go of past pain—inner pain that forms the basis for trauma-based words or actions. Through being "reborn," many people have gone on to live successful lives.
- Christians are reminded that God is love and that one of their main paths in life was to strive to love those who they find hard to love. This hard to love person may well have been, from time to time, their spouse.
- The Bible encourages monogamous marriage and responsible, respectful use of our sexual nature. Thus, the wedding vows of the Church of England state the following: -

Dearly beloved... duly considering the causes for which Matrimony was ordained: -
First, it was ordained for the procreation of children, to be brought up in the fear and nurture of the Lord, and to the praise of his holy Name.

> *Secondly, it was ordained for a remedy against sin, and to avoid fornication; that such persons as have not the gift of continency might marry, and keep themselves undefiled members of Christ's body.*
>
> *Thirdly, it was ordained for the mutual society, help, and comfort, that the one ought to have of the other, both in prosperity and adversity.*

All the above does not mean that the cultures that the Christian worldview created were perfect. It is just that Christian nations have been eminently sustainable and have provided the opportunity for future development. They have developed over many centuries because the Christian worldview aligned itself so well with our natural-family norms—norms that encouraged citizens to act as responsible adults and grow to be better at being fully human. Thus, in 1835, the writer Alexis de Tocqueville supposedly said the following after visiting America.

> *I sought for the greatness and genius of America in her commodious harbors and her ample rivers—and it was not there; in her fertile fields and boundless forests—and it was not there; in her rich mines and her vast world commerce—and it was not there; and in her democratic Congress and her matchless Constitution—and it was not there. Not until I went into the churches of America and heard her pulpits flame with righteousness did I understand the secret of her genius and power. America is great because she is good, and if America ever ceases to be good, she will cease to be great.*

It is not just the Christian faith that has been able to do this. Other religions have similar themes. All the major religions have ideas running through them that allow the followers to harmonize, to a greater or lesser extent, with our species norm. That is why these faith-based cultures have survived for so long. For example, Judaism has endured through upheaval and persecution solely because the core of the Old Testament seeks to inspire the Jews to grow the skills and attitudes that allow for the building of supportive communities of marital families. If Judaism had focused on the worshipping of nature or animal sacrifice, it would have died out long ago.

Moreover, the core tenants of Confucianism focus on developing oneself to create harmony within the marital-family home and society. Islam has similar elements. If the scriptures of these faiths gave rise to a far less comprehensive worldview, these faiths would have died out long ago—just as many other religions have done.

Today's Western societies face a complex challenge. Many of the young say something like, "I can be a good person without religion." And this is true. However, from a cultural-longevity perspective, people need a worldview that keeps them attached to our optimal species-norm across generations. Moreover, the young do not realize that when they leave behind the Christian worldview of their ancestors, they leave themselves open to being persuaded that we do not have a species norm. Alternatively, they might be told that we have a completely different species norm. Failure of development and decay will be the natural outcome, but this will take some time to see.

The fact that, throughout history, religions have been the primary channel through which humans have remained somewhat connected to our species norm is a complex issue. In an age where many people feel they don't want to be part of an organized religion, the question then needs to be asked as to how the wider society can become the core channel through which we are all reminded of our natural heritage.

More than this, many today have become disconnected from the lives of their ancestors. Many now connect the call for sexual control and the appeal to marriage as something that is solely associated with an established religion. They do not see the link between religious scriptures and our species norms. How does one talk to the modern young adult about abstaining from sex before marriage—a practice that all the truelove arctic terns and gibbons believe is essential for the well-being of their species—without being told you are simply a religious fanatic? It is a complicated time for any young adult growing up in such a confusing world. Seeking abstinence was a fundamental truth that almost everyone in the West understood some hundred years ago. And citizens understood this truth not because their religion told them, but because they saw the extremely negative results that could happen to a woman or a community that went down that path.

On our most fundamental level, we cannot escape our species norms. We are a lasting-love species, and, as such, a three-blessings lifestyle is our norm. If we try to pretend we are something different, we harm both our citizens and our nations in the long run.

Social Institutions And Our Species Norm

Through my extensive research, I have come to believe that our societies are likely to flourish through following the norms of the other lasting-love animals. This means that the primary function of all the leading social institutions—the political realm, the education system, businesses, the courts, religions, and the media—should be to support citizens on their way to the fulfillment of their three-blessings lifestyle. It is in the interest of our democratic, Western civilization that people develop into wholesome citizens, into successful partners in marriage, and into employees or entrepreneurs who can create a thriving economy.

If one looks at the data from all post-Christian nations today, it is easy to see how the marital-family norm has been neglected from the social discussion. A negative feedback loop has set in. With the norm of marriage not being supported by social institutions, all these institutions eventually suffer harmful outcomes.

- Today, without the education system fully supporting our natural family norm, increasing numbers of children with behavioral or psychological issues cause immense challenges for the schools.

- When businesses fail to support the family system, many of their employees struggle to be productive. A divorcing employee, or one who regularly struggles at home, might be able to give only 50 percent of their abilities at work. Stress causes many days of sick leave. Also, with so many of today's children having suffered lineage decline, it is harder for companies to find capable employees. Furthermore, the loss of moral integrity, which often inflicts itself on the social fabric as the family system fractures, can cause immense costs to businesses in a wide range of ways.
- When the political realm fails to support the marital-family norm, the nation can only suffer decline, both morally and financially.
- When a faith community does not focus on supporting the marital families of the faithful, divorce is more common. Divorcees are more likely to walk away from their faith.

One might ask, "If there was a king of the truelove swans, would he have any right to pass a law giving all swans the liberty to separate from their marital partner if they were struggling with each other?" We all know that if this happened, though the cygnets would not have to endure the pain of their parents' disagreements, they would be less protected from predators. Also, by herself, the mother would be less able to fight for the best feeding areas. Thus, the offspring would be more likely to suffer untimely deaths. The cygnets would also be less likely to inherit the good traditions that both parents embody. Thus, we can all realize that in passing such a policy, the swan species as a whole would be more prone to decay than development. In staying together despite their relationship challenges, the swans have survived for millions of years.

Once we realize this, one then has to ask a serious question. Do our elected political representatives have any natural right to pass laws that cause us to forget that we are a truelove species or create legislation that undermines the inner elements that support the functioning of the three blessings? Do they have any natural right, having been voted in to improve social outcomes, to do the exact opposite? Do they, some temporarily-elected officials or our judiciary, own our species norm, thus allowing them to do what they like with it? Or is our species norm owned by all citizens—past, present, and future? Is it there for the mutual benefit of all communities across history?

The Natural Rights Of Humans

Once one understands that we follow the norms of the lasting-love species, then it is possible to create an understanding of our human rights. If our lives and societies can only flourish if we fulfill our three inherited obligations, then human beings need the freedom to pursue these inherent responsibilities. We derive our natural rights from our three-blessings norm—rights that apply to us all.

If we call them natural rights, it is easier to understand what they are. In my understanding, natural rights exist to create optimal and sustainable outcomes for present and future generations. This is how nature works for all species. Mother Nature is into future sustainability. If the State takes away any of our natural rights, worse outcomes come about for future generations. Sadly, over the last sixty years, politicians and judges have done precisely this.

Also, natural rights exist to keep us grounded and connected to the natural world. If we disconnect ourselves from the natural world, then our brains can drift off into a fantasy world where we start to create all kinds of invented realities. That may be fine for a science-fiction movie or a horror story. However, in truth, our relationship with the physical world is an essential part of our well-being. We call rights "natural" because we derive them from our bond with the physical world, from our relationship with our physical bodies, and from the reality that we can create biological children.

Based on the three-blessings norm, we can say that all humans have the following natural rights.

- I have a natural right to pursue my goal to become a mature, fruitful individual.
- I have a natural right to be free to marry to best protect and nurture my biological children.
- I have a natural right to start a business or seek work to earn an income and take care of myself and my family's financial needs.
- Like a puffin, I have a natural right to keep most of the money I make with my talents.
- I have a natural right to connect with my extended family, my friends, and my faith community as supportive resources for my personal growth and family life.
- I have a natural responsibility, and thus a natural right, to take care of the environment for future generations.
- Like everyone else, I have a natural right to protect myself and my family from aggression, and an equal right to say what I believe to be true.
- In general, we all have a natural right not to be forced to pay off someone else's debt.

Children also have natural rights. We know children have intrinsic rights because we make it illegal to sell them at the ages of five or ten. In essence, children have a right to a childhood that doesn't seriously harm their ability to fulfill their three-blessings birthright.

- Children have a natural right and desire to be raised, if it is at all possible, by their two biological parents.
- Babies and children, like everyone else, have an equal right to life.
- Children also have a natural right to expect adults to protect them from the abusive desires and behaviors of other adults.
- Like everyone else, children have a natural right to be free from slavery—free from the painful thought that they were bought and sold to fulfill someone else's needs.
- Because of the above, the core sentence that drove the development of our Christian nations was, "We, parents, will

sacrifice our happiness to make a better future for our children."

All the above constitute our primary natural rights as humans. When our communities afford us these rights, and we seek to use them to fulfill our inherent responsibilities, our societies flourish. If politicians wish to build healthy nations, they would be best advised to uphold these natural rights within the legal framework.

There is a crucial point to understand here. The natural responsibilities and rights that we have been given all exist as a means to create optimal outcomes for our families and communities. In practice, this means that if any natural right is taken away, then this is akin to taking away a natural responsibility. In other words, when natural rights are lost, citizens start to feel less responsible. Then, citizens begin to feel less connected to our species norm, and social damage sets in.

The core underlying principle here is that "When a natural right is taken away, even for the sake of a seemingly good cause, then this will create future social damage. Suppose our political representatives or the judiciary take away natural rights from one group in society to presumably help another. In this case, the harm created will be far more extensive than the good that the politicians or judiciary originally hoped to achieve."

In not understanding this natural law, a nation can go into a spiral downwards. A natural right is taken away in the name of helping one social grouping. Future damage occurs. Then, twenty years later, legislators feel compelled to take away even more natural rights to support the new groups of struggling citizens. And then, even more damage occurs. A spiral downwards arises. The challenge is to learn to see the increased level of future harm. It is always there.

The Story Of Our Humanity

The story of our species tells a tale of a force beyond the human world, which created a boy and a girl who were destined to fall in love. Both strive to become wholesome and mature young adults. They meet and become good friends. They go through a courtship dance to see if the other might be "the one." They do not involve themselves in pre-marital sex because they know this will confuse them and even possibly cause them harm. Eventually, they marry and have children. Through their love and the love of other marital families, they create a community of friendship and support. They all raise their children together in goodness, teaching them how to fashion joyful lives. And they work to pay their way through life. But they know they live within boundaries that ask them to treat their sexuality with respect, so they stay sexually faithful to each other. Also, they know they can only achieve their goal of becoming one in love if they keep growing and learning about the finer points of love and affection. They know that for things to work, they must learn to be open to guidance from other significant people in their lives—their parents, friends, and relatives, and from their connection with the divine or their inner conscience. There is simply no better way to protect and raise children. We cannot change this best-outcomes human story or equation. Thus, Jordan Peterson made the following comments about how he believes nations stay healthy.

> *There is a way out (of the problem that we tend to support hurtful ideologies out of fear of persecution and isolation). It's the way out genuinely religious people have tried to offer humanity for thousands of years. It's the personal development of a truly powerful and integrated character. This means constant attempts to ensure that your character is composed of truth and solidity rather than deceit. I fully believe that every time you make a pathological decision, you move the world one step closer to annihilation. I also believe that every time you make an appropriate moral decision, or you manifest moral courage in the face of your own*

vulnerability, then you move the world one step away from the brink. And that's the case for every single person. We are all a "center of the cosmos." Our individual moral decisions affect everyone on earth.

As we become more technologically powerful, an increasing moral burden is being imposed on each of us. It matters to the destiny of the cosmos whether you get your moral act together. And I don't mean this in a trivial way. Maybe it's too much to ask of people. But our religious traditions do continually remind us that inside each one of us lies a spark of divinity. This belief underlies our entire legal system. If this is true, then, inside every single person, there is an infinite amount of potential. We each have the ability to transform the terrible conditions of reality into something that is not only acceptable but worthy of celebration.

All animals recognize that once they have chosen their sexual and family norms, they must stick with them. Our three-blessings natural-family story was determined for us long ago. If we follow this norm out of individual conscience, our societies experience the best possible futures. We cannot change this. This is our reality.

Of course, we will never reach the point where no citizens divorce, or no partners commit infidelity, or all couples marry, or no dating couples have pre-marital intercourse. However, just because we will never reach this point does not mean we cannot do much better than we already are.

Historically, the world has seen far more polygamous cultures than monogamous ones. But, for two thousand years, Christians in Europe have been at the very heart of an extended social experiment. They have been trying to use the above story, to a greater or lesser extent, as the basis for the growth of their nations. It was a long social experiment to rejoin our natural-family story—to see if, through the energy they created together, one man and one woman, could create a sustainable, developing society. To make this experiment work, they needed the help of a book that they believed was inspired by a universal power.

Step by step, Europe grew to be an island of creativity in an often, far-from-creative world. Europe and the U.S. rose to be places where there was a growth of democracy and growing respect for the rights of citizens. Was it a comfortable journey? No, it was not. Sometimes the religious authorities made the journey harder than it should have been, but religiously inspired individuals and groups brought about many positive changes.

The words in the Bible, in general, embodied developmental energy, which is why people all over Europe adopted it as a means to build social stability and lay the foundation for growth. The guidance on sexual and marital norms sought to minimize the risk of harm to children and, instead, tried to focus the minds of adults on behaviors that built a brighter future through the process of lineage development.

4. AN EXPLORATION OF THE THIRD BLESSING

The Fundamental Rules Of The Third Blessing

I have previously made the case that the optimal economic model for humans is the same one that guides the lives of the responsible puffins. The four basic principles include: -

- The integrity of individuals, the legal system, businesses, and politicians (almost no sharks).
- Uphold the natural rights of individuals and companies—that they get to keep most of the money that their abilities and skills create
- Politicians and communities endeavor to support the economic environment—roads, laws, education, etc.
- Do not destroy the eco-system that feeds us.
- The natural, primary purpose of economic life is to uphold each citizen's natural right and duty to strive to develop their talents so they can house and feed themselves and their family.

It was under this framework that the Christian West grew. There was no welfare system in place, but still, Europe and the U.S. developed. In general, those who contributed the most useful ideas and products became successful. Those who invested in their education or worked hard were more likely to be rewarded for their initiative. There was a natural feedback loop that rewarded good behavior. In a society with a reasonably fair legal system, those who lived more ethical lives typically found their families did better than those who did not.

However, from the 1930s onward, social welfare policies started to be developed. These policies began to infer that there was no way of improving the social fabric so that those who were currently experiencing economic hardship could be lifted out of their difficulties by raising the level of human wholesomeness and striving for excellence. In this legislative intervention, the State deemed it acceptable to take money from some families and give it to others. A violation of natural rights in the name of compassion began. However, the process of taking away rights from citizens always brings about future decay. Thus, all nations with a long Christian heritage have now endured ever-increasing levels of taxation, ever-growing national debts, and many are now having to experience years of austerity when it comes to public spending.

None of this has to be. These nations were once consistently developing under more natural laws and can succeed once again.

Singapore Follows A Natural And Sustainable Path

We can compare the social welfare model of Europe and the U.S. to a nation that went in a completely different direction, Singapore. In the 1960s, Singapore became an independent nation. The new leader, Lee Kuan Yew (LKY), believed that human beings, when allowed to live in a supportive economic eco-system, were overwhelmingly capable of taking care of their own financial needs. Under such a philosophy, LKY was recognized for transforming his nation from a third world nation to a first world nation in little over two generations.

Singapore took a very different approach than Europe. Sixty years ago, the government decided to force every worker to save from the moment they started work. Thus, everyone would have money to draw upon to get through any financial-challenging moment of their life. For many years now, both workers and employers have been legally required to make substantial contributions into three separate saving funds. Rather than paying high rates of taxation, citizens save. Thus, the personal taxation rates for individuals (i.e., about 10 percent if one earns about one hundred thousand dollars) and the sales tax of 7 percent are exceptionally low for a developed nation. Instead, the law requires citizens to save about 25-30 percent of their salary, and their company then pays roughly the same into these savings accounts. The State says. "You can create your retirement fund, or pay for your children's university education, or your health insurance, or a large part of your doctor's visit, and more. This is not our job. We do not want large numbers of people to be dependent on the finances of others. You are capable and noble." These saving accounts consist of: -

- The Ordinary Account (OA)—citizens save up for their own house or their child's future education, and so they have extra finances on retirement (CPF). This fund can also be topped up by the government—for example, six to ten thousand dollars for the birth of a child (Baby Bonus) and support for the education of lower-income families (EduSave)
- The Special Account (SA) for old age and investment in retirement-related financial products
- The Medisave Account (MA) for hospitalization and approved medical insurance

From a species-norms perspective, there are many benefits to such a system, for example: -

- While many young adults in other developed democracies are often using their money to enjoy the moment, young adults in Singapore are already being encouraged to think about their future marital and parenting path. Saving causes them to act and think like adults from the moment they start working.
- The system always keeps citizens in touch with their innate responsibilities.
- When people pay for their college degrees with the family's savings, they are more likely to choose professions that have social usefulness and are more committed to what they study.

In the data, we can see the effectiveness of this system of personal responsibility. It has raised the per capita income of citizens from about five hundred dollars a year some fifty years ago to some fifty-two thousand a year today—about 50 percent higher than Britain's. The average annual growth rate of the Singapore economy has been 7 percent since 1970. Furthermore, the UK social welfare system and the Singaporean "you are quite capable of looking after yourself" model produced vastly different State budgets. There are almost no social welfare costs in Singapore, and health expenditure only accounts for some 14 percent of public spending.

Conversely, health and social protection now account for over 50 percent of the UK's public spending, and this increases every year. Sadly, in the UK, broader economic growth is severely stifled by the system's abnormal demands. One of the other key differences between the two countries is that Singapore spends far more money on strengthening and supporting marriages. It is good to support citizens to get things right, not just pick up the pieces.

One of the core reasons for Singapore's success was that LKY pushed for a high standard of honesty both in the civil service and the wider business community. He clearly understood the link between integrity and receiving economic blessings. As a result, Singapore now ranks near the top of Transparency International's league table, showing itself to be an overwhelmingly trustworthy place to do business.

The result is that around 90 percent of Singapore's citizens own their homes, and many become millionaires. Also, because the whole system encourages a sense of personal responsibility: -

- There is very little crime—around 400 crimes per 100,000 citizens per year compared to 10,000 in Sweden (the world leader in the social-welfare model). In the UK, person-to-person violence is continuing its relentless rise.
- It has a low divorce rate, about 14 percent compared to Sweden's 45 percent.
- The suicide rate is 8 in 100,000 citizens compared to Sweden's 13.
- The homicide rate is one-third of Sweden's.

- Because of stricter drug laws, there is almost no drug abuse.
- The Singapore government has healthy savings in the bank and no debt.

One might say that forcing people to save as soon as they get their first job is a slightly authoritarian stance for any government to take. However, taking money from responsible families and giving it to ones that act less responsibly to gain political power is even more authoritarian. Such behavior is also much more prone to abuse by politicians who end up promising what they cannot sustainably deliver. The Singapore government is not asking citizens to give their money away but to act like adults—to save for the rainy days. All Nordic countries demand that both employees and entrepreneurs save for their pension. Such a system protects everyone because each citizen's pension is not dependent on how much the State can afford to give at a later date. The Singapore government takes this concept and stretches it further into health and higher education. It encourages citizens to do what they would naturally do for themselves if they realized what lay ahead.

The politicians fully believe that citizens, with the right support, can take care of their own lives. They also believe that citizens have a natural duty to act in ways that respect the natural rights of others. In practice, this means that the government can come down very hard on anyone who seeks to break the law and harm others. It also means citizens are never financially disconnected from the public services they receive. For example, depending on their level of income, each citizen is asked to pay a substantial amount of their medical bills from their savings or have health insurance in place. And when citizens sense that these are their essential responsibilities, and the government creates a legal framework that supports their natural responsibilities, the overwhelming majority choose to live by this standard. They see how they all are pulling together to make Singapore a vibrant place to live. Over 70 percent of voters voted to keep the present government in power in the last free and open election.

Singapore has become an attractive place to live because it seeks to honor, to a reasonable degree of integrity, many of the natural laws that lay the foundation for a society to receive blessings. The Buddhist-Confucian mindset of most Singaporeans, a philosophy formulated mainly in China, values education, thrift, family cohesion, and hard work. Hong Kong also has experienced incredible levels of growth using the same mentality and the same low-tax regime. Unsurprisingly, it is a worldview with many similarities to the one that Puritanism gave rise to in Great Britain and the Lutherans used to construct the Nordic countries.

Among the many other examples of the economic success that comes with a low tax regime, one can look to the early years of Islam. Islam spread rapidly across N. Africa in the eighth century, in part because the Islamic leaders promised that those who converted to Islam would not have to pay the poll tax. This lack of taxation led to a strong spirit of entrepreneurship, which led to Islam's golden years. Rapid technological development occurred, and citizens built magnificent buildings.

The Nordic countries and Singapore have many similar cultural norms. However, the fact that the Finnish State has created a national health service, a benefit system that encourages single parenting, and also offers free university places with generous student grants means that they have high taxes. They are violating one of the foundational rules of the third blessing. Therefore, their national debt is out of control, and public expenditure is unsustainable.

Along with a low tax regime, Singapore has also pursued excellence as a means to ensure that as many citizens as possible live somewhat successful lives. Singapore University has some of the best science departments on Earth, a stunning achievement for such a small nation. Its children come close to the top of the educational tables. In its pursuit of integrity, it has become one of the prime banking centers of Asia.

Thus, in low-tax Singapore, most citizens have enough money to build comfortable lives. Because of the self-sufficient attitude and the legislation that supports it, the State only needs to employ some 4 percent of the total national workforce. In the UK, the government hires some 16 percent of the national workforce. The costs involved in collecting, managing, and often giving back these taxes to those who they were taken from are vast. A substantial percentage of State employees are contributing nothing to increase the GDP. The drain on economic growth is enormous. This means that the UK can only manage an average increase in GDP of 2.4 percent compared with Singapore's 7 percent. The weakening of the social fabric that follows means that, today, almost 50 percent of the UK population needs some form of financial assistance from public finances. In essence, high rates of taxation cause far more damage than they supposedly fix. Thus, Thomas Sowell made the manifestly truthful comment.

> *It is amazing that people who think we cannot afford to pay for doctors, hospitals, and medication somehow think that we can afford to pay for doctors, hospitals, medication, and a government bureaucracy to administer it.*

Of course, when it comes to the arena of the third blessing, there are benefits to having some level of taxation. There needs to be protection, some nurturing, and the development of infrastructure. However, eventually, there comes a time when a higher level of taxation violates the natural law of citizens being able to keep most of their income. At this point, in a crude estimation, every one percent increase in taxation eventually leads to a one percent increase in struggling citizens—who ultimately have to seek financial support from public funds.

A nation can end up in a downward spiral, which is where our debt-laden post-Christian countries are at today. Today, the historically high taxation levels cause problems for many families—for families who would be amply self-sufficient in a low taxation environment. However, Singapore shows us that the State can embed principles into the legal framework so that, every year, fewer citizens need rescuing. The core difference between debt-ridden W. Europe and debt-free Singapore is political architecture.

Of course, Singapore is not perfect and has weaknesses that might well cause future weakening. For example, it has a low birth-rate and a growing number of divorces. In essence, the economic-freedom worldview that Singapore extols does not contain enough insights from our inherent species norm for Singapore to be sustainable, just by itself. It will have to rely on immigration. And the ongoing collapse of marriage will slowly but surely create problems for future generations to come. But still, as a nation, it has become a remarkable showcase that other countries can learn from.

In summary, by striving for excellence and requiring that citizens save for the rainy days, Singapore can build a flourishing and protective nation with a total tax regime (i.e., personal and sales tax) of less than 20 percent. Other countries are surprisingly inefficient when they try to become all things to all people through high rates of taxation.

Mormonism Shows Us A Faith-Based Model

Singapore shows us a model that can be used to create a flourishing society without an overbearing State. However, it is not the only model available. For example, as a faith community, the Mormons of Utah have found a way to build communities that can support most families and individuals as they experience various challenges on their path through life. No large State bureaucracy is needed.

The Mormons follow a story that the Book of Mormon gives rise to. This story is quite well aligned with our species norm. Pre-marital sex is strongly discouraged, and the divorce rate is considerably lower than other Christian-aligned denominations. Also, their communities have a flourishing birth rate.

Because of their story's inherent strengths, the Mormons in Utah have built up an impressive list of community resources for supporting their families through community tithing and donations. For example, they purposely run companies that are designed to provide temporary jobs for the unemployed. If you are struggling in your marriage or with your children, expert assistance is there to help. They have a well-designed School of Family Life at Brigham Young University—a department that provides useful resources to strengthen the faithful's marital families. Moreover, they have free food shops for those who are in need. None of this needs big government. In return for a 10 percent tithe on their income, the faithful get an impressive suite of support systems. Through creating such thoughtful structures, communities have far fewer families crying out for help. Because of the Mormon Church's family-focused activities, Utah now tops all other American states on almost every aspect of family well-being.

The community aspect of the Mormon church has many similarities to other Christian communities that have proved to be eminently sustainable. For example, the Amish communities in the U.S. have shown themselves to be family resilient and socially oriented. Other church communities have done the same.

Above, I have made the case that our nations do best when we each fulfill the responsibilities that come within the remit of our lasting-love species norm. Such a worldview sees each family fulfilling their obligations within their unique family home. However, this in no way invalidates the idea of communities of families voluntarily working together to create a supportive community. By far and away, building a community of support is far more preferable than the concept of individual families just living their lives in separation. Supportive community-living harkens back to the time when we lived in small villages, and almost everyone was involved in both family and community life. And look where we are today because we reached out.

However, today, in leaving the natural laws that bring blessings to our species, our post-Christian nations are almost all on course for economic and cultural suicide. For example, in the UK, the national health service, schools, and police struggle under ever-shrinking budgets. Every year, hundreds of thousands of crimes are no longer investigated by the overstretched police force.

Throughout history, one of the core problems has been: "How do we deal with citizens in challenging situations." To solve this problem, Western countries went down the pathway of increasing taxes. It hasn't worked. However, both Singapore and Mormonism have chosen pathways that lie within the remit of our species norm. As a result, they experience low rates of crime, they have found ways to protect the most vulnerable, lineage improvement is occurring in many people's lives, they are financially blessed, and positive social energy is an automatic outcome. These outcomes are not unique to only one or two groups of citizens. Blessings will come to any group that wishes to apply our species norms. We cannot change how blessings are created and how they drift away.

The Social Fabric Through Legislators' Eyes

The world of the trueloves is one where each person and their family live a noble life that is predicated on consistent learning, growth, self-sufficiency, and resourcefulness. The energy of the species lies within the individual development of each person, within the skills that the partners bring to their marital family, and in each individual's ability to develop their skills to flourish economically. All this is predicated on the individual's desire to fulfill their responsibilities as a means to build a thriving community.

Our natural-family norm makes it very clear that it is not the job of political representatives to disconnect individuals or a marital family from their inherent responsibilities. The natural law of personal responsibility always needs to be upheld within the legal framework. Lineage improvement happens when we all grow through taking responsibility. The struggles we experience often show that individual growth is needed. If that growth takes place, then individuals become more competent, lineage improvement might occur, and social problems will lessen. If they step in at the wrong time, our political representatives can stop this growth from happening. Stagnation and decay are then a distinct possibility.

In the natural world, the parent swans raise their young to self-sufficiency through using three core personas. They nurture and teach them. They seek to be protectors of their offspring. And they ensure their well-being by choosing and creating a suitable environment to raise them in. These three personas also relate to the human world, for they identify the three primary roles of our political representatives.

Politicians ideally focus on creating a social environment that protects citizens from the harmful acts of others (e.g., police, army, and judicial system). They need to promote the smooth running of community and economic life (e.g., town planning, road building, and a rational legislative framework). And they can create community-enhancing initiatives that give even the poorest the opportunity to raise themselves—thus allowing them the chance to protect themselves from some of the ravages of life (e.g., libraries, swimming pools, outdoor spaces that help citizens stay fit). It is in the context of offering free or affordable nurturing opportunities to all citizens that social policies become connected to our species norms.

Today, however, in many poorly-run democracies, the State has taken on the additional persona of being a rescuer. Rather than focusing on ensuring ever-fewer people end up needing to be rescued by community finances, many States now focus on creating a vast network of laws and procedures that do the exact opposite. Thus, the demand for increased levels of taxation is always heard. Dr. Ben Carson, who is presently part of the team that is seeking to revitalize cities across the U.S., clearly sees how state policies have caused much of the decline that afflicts many municipalities. He commented: -

> *We've been conditioned to think that only politicians can solve our problems. But at some point, maybe we will wake up and recognize that it was politicians who created our problems.*

Our politicians are not elected to rescue citizens. We select them to ensure that fewer citizens need rescuing. The political class needs to be clear that the most compassionate thing they can do is to encourage distinction—in personal, family, and work life.

People who strive for excellence do amazingly good things in the world. In their search for excellence, the mobile phone companies have done far more to raise the citizens of Africa out of poverty than all the billions of compassionate aid from Western nations ever did. If you are trying to find a builder to build your home, most of us would naturally choose a person with a rough character and a passion for craftsmanship over a person oozing with empathy but no passion for technical excellence. In most areas of life, we need primary values other than compassion and benevolence to be at work for things to work well.

When citizens develop their talents, they create new jobs, provide money for social renewal, push other professions to new levels, and encourage communities to find new ways to help underachievers so they can participate in an advanced society. The pursuit of excellence and truth in all walks of life is the optimal way to create a wholesome nation.

However, even though we solve social problems through the development of human beings, we can often find ourselves sidetracked. The demand for compassion can cause us to lose focus. We saw how this happened in the creation of the Soviet Union in 1917. Communism took over. The demand was that the leaders should care about the poor. In this demand for compassion and fairness, millions of managers and entrepreneurs were killed. The populace became frightened of striving for excellence in their economic life because, if they succeeded, they too might be shipped off to the gulags. The economy died as a result.

Meanwhile, in the democratic West, freedom and striving for excellence naturally lifted most of the poor out of dire poverty. Suburbs were built, and most people bought cars and washing machines. Life became comfortable for most. Meanwhile, behind the Iron Curtain, almost all citizens were struggling just above the poverty line, and social progress was near impossible.

Today, as the social-welfare model grows more expansive in our Western nations, the State grows larger. As this happens, it takes on more responsibility. As it takes on more responsibility, it takes on more power. As it takes on more power, then energy leaves the family system, and we move away from puffinism towards another species norm.

If one looks at the words of Jesus, he offered us clear advice on how a flourishing community is built. He talked about each person seeking distinction in their life as a means to benefit their community. He talked about using one's talents and money to help the poor and disadvantaged. He shared that not developing one's potential was something akin to a sin. However, he never mentioned the idea of having high taxes as a means to create a just and fair society. It is far too easy to use other people's money so you can feel good. You can sit in your armchair and personally do nothing. This is not what Jesus' message was about. It was about each of us finding an inner voice—asking us to do our bit to improve that which we were being called to improve. If we listen, we all are being called to do something more than just live for ourselves.

Yes, some small Christian communities have existed where people voluntarily shared economic resources. However, they are usually short-lived because such communities are prone to misuse and accusations. The early pilgrims who arrived in America tried community living but quickly gave it up. Furthermore, the Jews formed kibbutzim when they were re-establishing their nation in Israel during the 1960s. But, these also faded in popularity because they led to more problems than they solved. Today, many have switched to become communities where the families share common interests. Economically-driven communal living is not intrinsic to our natural species norm. But, in our complex world, building communities of mutual support can reap remarkable benefits.

What is the core issue here? When, as a means to solve a social problem, money is forcibly taken from some families and given to other families, this act sets a puffin-valuing nation on a pathway towards living under a different species norm. When we try to live under a different species norm, our nations go into decay.

Therefore, our political representatives need to think about how they can support the development of citizens so they can build sustainable marital families and successful careers. Rescuing is a matter for charities, family systems, and insurance companies. Charities and family systems have the time and energy needed to help struggling individuals get back on track. Companies can help too, for example, through apprenticeship schemes, charitable giving, and sponsoring schools.

The primary role of legislators who have inherited a democratic tradition is to keep the power of a nation within the realm of the family system. Free from the unnatural interventions of State bureaucracy, humans can build friendships, become part of a community of faith, and can create resilient family networks to help them as they seek to succeed in their three-blessings lifestyle. The State does not have to believe that it needs to become all things to everyone, and then eventually fail when trying to achieve something that it was never designed to achieve. A nation becomes the best it can be when we are all supported on our path to become the best we can be.

5. ON HUMAN WHOLESOMENESS

Mind And Body Unity

In chapter three, I remarked that individual growth was one of the three primary channels through which humans increased their ability to receive blessings. I also noted that the foundation for all species to thrive was built upon the desire of each individual to strive to embody a sense of wholesomeness based on the norms of their species.

Like all species, we develop towards our full potential through the interplay between the mind and our body. The concept of human wholesomeness not only covers how we think with our brain but how we act with our physical body.

How we manage the interaction between these two main aspects of our being will determine much of our lives. I might neglect my body and suffer negative consequences as a result. Some of us ignore the development of our minds, and, therefore, our lives might be less fulfilling than we hoped. Some of us focus on developing some parts of our mind to a high level of competence and become experts who bless the world with new ideas or well-run companies. And, a person can use their brain to develop some aspect of their body to a high level of competence. Thus, ballerinas enchant the world with their grace, athletes thrill us, and the craftsman who builds a delightful custom car can inspire us.

Because there is circular give-and-take action between our mind and body, energy is created. This energy means that humans build houses, create products, and paint paintings. Thus, we develop our world, transforming food energy into creative energy, which leads to inventive outcomes.

It is not only my world that I build when I create something. The interaction between my mind and my body also generates social energy. This energy then ripples out into our families and communities. Each of our acts might lead to the continued existence, sustainability, and development of our culture or, conversely, our actions can lead to the eventual deaths of our culture. For example, an addiction that resides within one member of a family system can have a profoundly negative effect on the extended family and beyond. Or a legal decision by a single judge or politician can change the behavior of millions of citizens, for the better or worse.

Of course, some acts have more significant implications than others. But still, a healthy culture is one where the overwhelming majority of citizens decide to act in ways that lead to ongoing social well-being.

Along with many other issues, mind and body unity is also the basis of building interpersonal and social trust. If I say I will meet my friend at eight o'clock, and then turn up at eight, my behavior builds trust. When we talk and sign a contract, and the agreement is upheld, positive energy is then manifested. If a scientific formula works in practice, we know we can design and build a bridge with it without causing social harm. If a law is passed, but that law does not seem to apply to the rich and famous, then social decay is inevitable. Thus, personal integrity, which is built into the mind and body dynamic, is also a core element of a flourishing community.

Because of this reality, we all—no matter our race, faith, sex, or background—stand at the center point of good or evil. We all can, at every second of the day, make decisions that have a much higher chance of creating positive outcomes. Thus, we return to the concept of the first blessing. Those who seek to behave in ways that generate positive social energy are much more likely to sense their life is blessed compared to those who act in ways that create socially-harmful outcomes.

Today, a child can enter into a vast array of sports and hobbies as a means to increase their level of mind and body coordination and as a means to understand what might uplift or harm their lives. However, underneath all the sports, hobbies, and intellectual development is the underlying theme that all truelove species encounter. The central question is always, "How can the young enter into adulthood with the skills needed to ensure the success of their offspring and the ability to provide for their own or their family's economic needs?"

I previously noted that for the truelove species, the concept of wholesomeness could only be maintained based on certain core principles.

- The ability of the new generation to recognize and inherit the good of the past—the essential behaviors, core values, traditions, and attitudes that had kept their species resilient in previous generations
- The self-development drive—the individual desire to set oneself on a path that leads to ongoing growth and mastery

There is also the central purpose of the first blessing. It seems that we ultimately wish to know that we have achieved some level of mastery over various aspects of life itself—that we have created far more positive social energy than negative. At the end of our lives, many of us express sincere regret when our life has not been as fruitful as we would have liked it to be.

Because cooperation between our mind and our body is at the very core of the human experience, it is worth looking at various aspects of what it means to be an individual who is living in a community in relation to our species norm.

Core Values

All lasting-love species live by specific core values that are essential to the well-being of their families and communities. The focus is on doing an honorable job in my family while leaving other individuals to fulfill their natural responsibility in theirs. These core values include: -

- The young puffin appears to respect the values, traditions, and the good that is shown to them by their parents.
- They rarely kill those of their own species.
- By staying away from infidelity, they strive to not cause problems for other families.
- Through not stealing from each other, they strive to not cause problems for other families in their communities.
- Through focusing purely on their own responsibility, they seem to naturally stay away from comparing their family situation to other families. Jealousy is not part of their norm.

The astute reader will recognize the Biblical connection here. At the start of the Judaic faith, God gave the descendants of Abraham ten commandments that they would be wise to follow if they wished to build lasting communities. Because we are truleoves, the core values are the same as those that the puffins use. The focus is on one's responsibility and not harming other families to benefit yourself or your family.

When looking at the natural world, the core values mentioned above are not essential to the lives of many other species. Lions will kill the offspring of another male to bring a lioness back into heat. When a lion does this, he does not harm the natural mating habits of his species. If truelove males did the same thing, our family systems would quickly become highly dysfunctional.

Also, wolves will kill a wolf from another pack. However, unlike many veterans of the war in Afghanistan, they carry on with their lives without any hint of PTSD. Lastly, in some monkey troupes, the older females will encourage the young teenage males to copulate with them. No psychological harm is done. No guilt. No shame.

In summary, the ten commandments stand as a timeless channel through which humans bring blessings into their communities.

Love and Beauty

In the human species, there is one core dynamic that drives all healthy personal development and the growth of all enriching relationships. This dynamic also pervades all things we enjoy about life. And it is essential in the lives of the trueloves. This dynamic might be called the "love and beauty" dynamic.

At the heart of the enduring relationships of the lovebirds and the cranes is a deep sense of mutual appreciation. The male sees the beauty and goodness in the female. Likewise, she sees the goodness and beauty in him. His appreciation of her goodness triggers a natural force—a power that encourages him to keep giving into their relationship. The same for her. Since they are both triggered to offer something more into their relationship, they end up appreciating each other even more. After they have both given something good into their family life, then, after a long day of giving, they snuggle up next to each other and feel as though life is good. Thus, the interaction between "giving love" and "sensing the beauty" draws the couple into an energy-creating dynamic that manifests itself in the world. This energy allows them to participate in life, to want to grow, and to create a family together.

Because we are trueloves, we have the same types of drugs and wiring in our brains that support the love and beauty dynamic. When we find beauty in our spouse, we are triggered to enter into a deeper relationship. Also, we seek to create new things so that we can feel pride in the beauty that we can manifest. Moreover, it is the energy that is created through the love and beauty dynamic that is the "food" our soul needs so that we can consistently raise ourselves up to a higher level of competence and wholesomeness. The dynamic offers vitality to our life.

For the sake of simplicity, one might say that humans perceive beauty in a wide range of ways. We find beauty in doing something meaningful, in seeking and finding truth, in seeing goodness, in experiencing joy, and in beauty itself. Our search for truth triggers a surge in energy, inspiring us to search and grow. The desire to create a meaningful life pushes us to build families and do useful work. Our sense of appreciation for beauty causes us to redecorate our homes or drags us around the world to see nature's or humankind's handiwork. We control our behavior or do acts of kindness to fulfill our inner need to sense we are good. And we like it when we immerse ourselves in joyfulness. The interplay between the giving of ourselves into life and our desire to appreciate beauty in all its different forms creates the energy that drives human life itself.

If we find some form of meaning in the task we are doing, then this triggers us to give more of ourselves into that task. If we find a job to be meaningless, our energy level wanes. If we meet someone for the first time, and we find it easy to see goodness in this person, we are far more likely to give of ourselves into the relationship. If we find beauty in an object or a work of art, we want to bring it into our lives. Each time we see it, it will remind us that the world is capable of goodness, allowing us to enter the world with a more positive attitude. Without having the ability to sense goodness, or beauty, or truth, or joy, or meaning, it would be hard for us to do anything more than seek to fulfill our most basic needs. When the desire to consistently enter into the love and beauty dynamic is present in the majority, an energy field that forms great cultures is created. Even long ago, this truth was clearly evident. For example, the Roman statesman, Marcus Cicero, noted, *"Gratitude is not only the greatest of virtues but the parent of all the others."*

Numerous pieces of research show us the value of gratitude. Appreciative people are, on average, more resilient, healthier, recover from illnesses and operations faster, find more joy in the small moments of life, and build stronger relationships. Hence, it is useful to know that we can all learn to look more deeply into ourselves, or others, or our nations, or a task, and appreciate more of the beauty that is intrinsically buried there.

Appreciation that triggers giving and giving that triggers appreciation is at the core of the parent-child relationship, our friendships, the boss-employee relationship, and the business-customer relationship. Also, when we realize that there is something beneficial to be learned from a challenge, we often generate the energy that is needed to sustain us through the educational process. Lastly, forgiveness plays an indispensable role in human relationships because it offers people the freedom to enter back into the love and beauty dynamic that is so essential for an enriching relationship and personal growth.

Despite the above, human beings are complex, and learning the art of appreciation takes time. Another challenge is that the universe has purposely designed us to be acutely aware of the things that might harm us. For our own self-preservation, we are much more aware of situations that might cause pain or adverse effects. This heightened sense of the difficulties of life causes a problem for us humans. For example, when a married couple argues, it takes more than one act of kindness to repair the psychological damage caused. It takes at least three acts of kindness to start to rebuild a sense of harmony. Because of this reality, research shows that happy couples seek to create at least five acts of appreciative kindness for every one disruptive moment.

A hundred years ago, G.K. Chesterton wrote of the joys of being grateful and what people who sought to continuously complain were missing out on. He wrote, *"I would maintain that thanks are the highest form of thought; and that gratitude is happiness doubled by wonder."*

Today, Westerners live in nations where most are much freer from the immense levels of suffering that their ancestors went through. Medicines and operations save our lives. Most of us have teeth. Almost all of us will live long lives. Most of us will never experience what it is like to lose several young children to disease or famine. Every day, billions of constructive moments of interaction take place between people of different races—at work or in friendships. Inter-tribal wars are not part of our daily reality.

Also, in the West, almost all have food to eat, warmth in our homes, and cars to drive. In our democracies, men and women enjoy levels of equality that are unheard of in human history. There is so much to be grateful for. All of us could have been born in a different era where life was a far more challenging experience. It is, therefore, essential that we all have a deep appreciation for the principles that have allowed such nations to be built.

The philosopher G.K. Chesterton once wrote, *"Gratitude, being nearest the greatest of human duties, is also nearly the most difficult."* He reminds us of something important. Appreciation for the good we have is not just something that is an optional extra. It is a duty, a natural responsibility of being a human within a community. We have an inherent obligation to seek to improve the communities we are part of, just as our ancestors did for us. However, just like a car producer cannot enhance a car without appreciating the good that is in the present generation of vehicles, we cannot seek to improve our nations if we do not value the goodness that our ancestors built into them. If we fail to look with appreciation, we might throw away some of the things that maintain the social good. We might throw away the brakes and airbags if we do not appreciate what they are there to do. We have a responsibility to make sure that we are not this foolish.

Why is it that the love and beauty dynamic is so fundamental to human well-being? Because it forms the basis for humans to have a relationship with God. God gives and seeks to appreciate the beauty in His children as a means to provide even more. And in return, humans ideally appreciate what they have received and seek to live a life that inspires God. There is no more beautiful dynamic that might inspire us to live an honorable life.

Because of the central role that the love and beauty dynamic plays in building healthy communities, if an enemy wanted to weaken a nation from within, there is no more of an effective way to do this than to destroy the next generation's sense of gratitude for the sacrifice of their ancestors and the blessings they have today.

In summary, appreciation and puffinism are intrinsically linked. If we lose our sense of thankfulness, we might lose our ability to connect with our species norm, and we will lose our democracies. The health of a nation is built upon the ability of citizens to notice the good that their country currently embodies and to understand how that goodness is maintained. On that foundation, improvements can then be made. However, today, who has been taught at school about the art of appreciation or forgiveness? We might lose our peace and security because we neglect such simple things.

The Divine Value Of The Individual

There are two fundamental reasons why the Christian West became so successful. First, there was freedom of speech, and thus, freedom to pursue truth. In continuously pursuing truth, new inventions and positive reforms were consistently made.

Second, there was the acknowledgment of the unique divinity of each person—with each adult being seen as personally responsible for their own behavior and each person being judged on their character. This is how it is in the realm of the trueloves. The health and well-being of the species are depended on the desire of each puffin to strive to become the most wholesome puffin they can be.

Because of the puffin-like mentality that Christianity gave rise to, our societies came to see each person as having equal responsibility to contribute to community life, and each person was judged on their own merits. This was different than countries like India, where the Hindu caste system saw each person as a member of a caste, and all were automatically judged based on the caste that they were born into. In doing so, the immense energy and gifts of talented individuals in the lower castes were denied. Growth slowed tremendously. Today, in the West, various groups of activists are working hard to create a caste-like way of viewing the social fabric. For example, in the U.S., there are the wise, Brahmin progressives and the untouchable deplorables, or the racist whites and the saintly souls of all other races. The negative repercussions of such falsehoods will harm the U.S. for years to come.

All the truelove species are not primarily group orientated. Each individual has a unique identity. Each has their responsibility, and their most profound meaning in life is found in fulfilling their three-blessings lifestyle.

Thus, the natural way of viewing each person is as a unique individual who has a noble responsibility to live life with dignity. We base our legal system on this fundamental principle. However, we all have to deal with a complicated ancestral history, one that is full of different forms of trauma. These traumas still have an impact on us today, making it harder for many of us to live the life we dream of living.

All of us have a family history that is filled with struggles and pain. Many families have lost wealth and loved ones in wars. Many of us have sexual abuse, suicide, or alcoholism within our family tree. Famines or epidemics have severely undermined the well-being of many of our ancestors. A considerable number of people today have been raised by a parent who had psychological problems to deal with, and now these individuals struggle with unwanted and harmful outcomes. None of us has a family tree that has not been oppressed by some group or another.

Moreover, when one looks at the history of masculinity, many men have lived lives oppressed by the challenges of life itself. Many died in coal mines or while fishing, and many became disabled while working with machinery. Also, countless men contracted life-shortening diseases from poor work conditions. It has always been that men died in wars or came back home without a limb or with severe mental health issues. Today, many males struggle because they had no father figure in their life. All these issues and more have had a grave, adverse effect on the ability of men to be as wholesome as women would like them to be.

Obvious, with such a history behind them, it is seriously ridiculous for the university system to call these men "toxic." Many males, if they receive some patient support from other men and women, can feel freer to live the noble life they wish to live. Only by working together are we going to have any hope of solving these issues.

The challenging situation of life itself has also caused the natural feminine nature of many women to become warped and traumatized. Many women in history have died during childbirth. Many experienced the heartache of watching their children die. Women of all races have experienced rape. We all have women in our family tree who have had to go through the difficult challenge of raising children alone and the trauma that this might have caused for the family system. Thus, yet again, women benefit from finding mutual support.

One of the complicated issues with traumas is that while they are stored within our subconscious, there is a higher chance that we will act in ways that will hurt others. In other words, behind a sinful act, there is often a hidden trauma at work. Thus, a person who was harmed as a child has a higher chance of harming others.

One can look back across the whole history of humankind and see that the everyday life experience of the majority of our ancestors was one of suffering and struggle. Just staying alive was hard. The wondrous divine nature of human communities is that, if they can start to live within the context of the three-blessings lifestyle, then, over the course of several generations, they can slowly reduce the number of daily struggles, and therefore, the number of traumatic incidents.

Also, the miracle of human beings is that despite our hidden traumas and grim past moments, most of us can still function to a reasonable level of competence. Despite the adverse effects these ordeals might have, most of us choose not to dwell on the negatives. Instead, most citizens pull themselves up by their bootstraps and try to do the best they can without seeking to claim victim status.

In reality, it is wholly impossible to say one form of historical hardship has been more harmful than another. In this honesty, each of us needs to be seen as an individual who is seeking to move away from this past damage, hoping to use their life to make their nation less prone to future suffering in whatever way they can.

Because of the truth of this reality, the Christian worldview pushes us to see each person as a unique child of God. We each have talents and a unique ancestral history of brokenness and trauma. We each have a personal responsibility to heal the emotional damage that is trapped within. No one else can do this for us. We either end up passing this trauma down to our children, or we set ourselves on a path towards healing and growth—thus improving the chance of bettering our own lives and our children's lives.

Such a perspective seeks to admire and honor those who strive to do their best to grow despite their historical baggage. Ideally, we become color or gender blind. We then decide for ourselves how much respect and trust we wish to offer the person in front of us, not based on some artificial political framework, but based on actual personal experiences.

In general, the three-blessings paradigm gives an honest assessment as to why, over time, some racial groups, cultures, or individuals succeed and why some do not. This assessment is based on how well individuals or cultures embodied various principles despite their suffering. In general, when individuals and cultures exemplify wholesome principles, then fewer moments of misery occur. The reality is that, in the West, we live in a time, no matter our past heritage, where we have the freedom to live a three-blessings lifestyle. And when we do this, we quite quickly see blessings building up within our family tree.

Thus, research on Americans and Europeans from any cultural background shows what happens when people live by tried and tested principles. Those who graduate high school, start working, get married, and have children—in that order—are significantly less likely to fall into poverty than those who follow a different life course. Studies show that these four core life choices, when sequenced together, provide the best path to a prosperous future. Ninety-seven percent of young adults who follow the success sequence are not living below the poverty line by the time they reach thirty. In particular, marrying before having children offers the most benefits.

Of course, some of us start from a more complex starting point. However, many citizens who come from a less complicated heritage can become ungrateful and complain, and thus refuse to enter into the love and beauty dynamic. With this attitude, their ability to grow is stifled and leaving the world a worse place than they found it is a distinct possibility. On the other hand, even those from a complicated heritage can build flourishing lives and admirable families. So much depends on the personal choices and attitudes of the individual. Only the individual can make this godlike decision, which will have a profound effect on the quality of their life. No matter how one's life started, it is always possible to make choices that will lead to a more fruitful life tomorrow. Our free societies offer this opportunity to all citizens. Many disadvantaged families from China or Korea have moved to America, and, through following healthy principles, they now see their children flourishing as doctors and lawyers.

One of the first stories in the Bible is of two brothers, Cain and Abel. Abel seems to make the right sort of sacrifices in his daily life, such that he receives blessings. On the other hand, his older brother Cain does not seem to be able to do what is needed to gain success. An angry Cain goes to God and complains. God responds,

"If you live by the right principles, then, of course, I will bless you." However, rather than learning to live those principles, Cain became resentful and killed his brother. Abel's success reminded Cain of his unwillingness to live a three-blessings lifestyle. Instead of continuously feeling judged by his brother's accomplishments, he decided to make his brother disappear.

Of course, there are many other issues here. For example, Jesus set an example of what it means to live a wholesome life. Though he was innocent of any crime, he was brutally and painfully murdered. As Jesus died, he asked God to forgive his murders. He fully understood that keeping resentment in one's heart would just perpetuate their harmful actions. Why should someone else's malicious act cause me to harm other innocent people today—thus causing me to destroy my own honor and life? Whatever the past, we all need to learn the art of forgiveness. In leaving behind past resentments, we become freer to build the kind of life we intrinsically desire. During the last century, for the sake of the well-being of their own lives and their national welfare, the English and French twice had to learn to forgive the Germans for killing off so many of their finest young men and women.

And, yet again, we almost all have negative memories when it comes to how our parents treated us as children. Many of us have had complicated childhoods. However, one of the most important steps we can take is to find those things that we can be grateful for in our youth—even if this just means appreciating the fact that we were given life itself. Often, without this gratitude-led forgiveness, many individuals find it harder to fully enter into the love and beauty dynamic that is life itself. They might hold back in fear, anger, or shame. However, the fact that we, if we so choose, can do such things shows us the divine, god-like capabilities of being human.

In summary, the hope is that each of us can sense that we are a unique individual with a complicated past, but born with the capacity to make a distinctive positive contribution to human history through any of the dimensions of the three-blessings framework. When we willingly take on this responsibility, we each become a center of the cosmos—enhancing the world that surrounds us for the sake of developing our own sense of honor and for the betterment of humankind.

Throughout history, people from very complex backgrounds have chosen to leave the past behind and, instead, live a nobler life. Thus, when people claim, or we claim, or others claim on behalf of others, that the burden of trauma is too heavy to bear—and thus personal change is impossible—this is a moment when deceit enters into the social fabric. And this is especially true in an era when we have multiple methods that might help individuals heal from the emotional wounds they have inherited from history.

When we accept such a lie, we take away all hope of ever building a world of peace. Why? Because we can then all blame history and our upbringing for our failings and never accept the responsibility that comes with being a human who is responsible for the destiny of the world. In saying, "My father was an alcoholic, and so were his father and grandfather—thus, I have to accept the fact that I am one too," leaves humanity in a hopeless situation. Our legal system, which is based on the workable idea of individual responsibility, would fall to pieces.

In this chapter, we examined some of the core elements that reside within the remit of the first blessing. We reviewed some of the key features that allow a person to sense that their life is blessed. Such a lifestyle involves taking on core values that enable us to protect our own sense of dignity and community life. Moreover, those who develop their sense of appreciation are much more likely to be drawn into living a life that wants to bring even more goodness, beauty, truth, joy, and meaning into the communities that inhabit this small heavenly sphere that we call earth.

Lastly, a world of peace and blessings comes about when each of us decides to connect to that divine spark that wishes for us to grow to become the best we can be. In a society where there are ample opportunities for personal growth and healing, we can all do a bit better than we are currently doing. I wish I had a dollar for every time I blamed others for my challenging situation—only to realize later that there were many things that I could have done that would have allowed me to move forward towards a more successful life. Blaming others just kept me blind to my own path of growth.

6. ONLY PUFFINS CAN BUILD DEMOCRACIES

The State's Interest In Marriage

It is worth asking why the State, in all Western democracies, had a specific interest in creating laws that supported the heterosexual marital-family. For sure, some three hundred years ago, with death in one's forties being commonplace, many widows or widowers lived together in friendship for many years. There were also people who, for one reason or another, never married. These singles might have lived with a friend across the whole of their life-span. But the State saw no reason to create laws around these enduring companionate relationships. Even if their relationships were caring, the State saw no need to develop legislation to support their adult-based relationships per se. If the State has no specific interest in regulating companionate relationships, then what was, and still is, of concern to the State when it seeks to support the heterosexual marital-family?

The State's interest was in the welfare of the children. For if children have a positive start in life, then future society will benefit. The State would ideally like to see as many children as possible raised by their two, committed, biological parents. The State is primarily interested in lineage development. With parents doing their job to a reasonable standard, and various elements of the social fabric supporting them in their parenting role, the State can then focus on developing and protecting the nation. The improved outcomes for children raised by their married biological parents were clear to see in an age before the welfare state. In 1996, some American politicians still clearly understood this reality when they wrote the American Defense of Marriage Act.

> *At bottom, civil society has an interest in maintaining and protecting the institution of heterosexual marriage because it has a deep and abiding interest in encouraging responsible procreation and child-rearing. Simply put, the government has an interest in marriage because it has an interest in children.*

It is this interest in child well-being that the State ideally represents in discussions with society concerning issues connected with sexuality, marriage, and the raising of children. It ideally seeks to uphold the fundamental natural rights of children.

- To protect the child from a whole range of demands by adults
- To ensure that as many children as possible are raised in the loving embrace of their two biological parents
- To ensure the child's natural right to life
- To not burden them with the debts of other citizens
- A natural right to be free from slavery—to be free from the trauma of having been sold by their biological mother or father

Children are best able to flourish when these natural rights are upheld within the culture and the law. If we are talking about long-term development, protecting children's rights has to be one of the crucial goals of our legislators. By taking this stand, the State guarantees lineage development, remains financially sustainable, and best protects its democratic ideals and future society. Thus, the Australian senator, Eric Abetz, wrote: -

> *Marriage is and has been a fundamental cornerstone of society. Its pre-existence of the nation-state, international treaties, and Supreme Courts places it in a unique and important social position. It reflects and upholds the biological and sociological realities of the family unit, and, as such, is the best and most effective system of raising, protecting, and socializing our next generation. For that, it deserves to be treated by society with the utmost respect.*

It is imperative to understand this concept. The State is interested in protecting the natural rights of the child. This is their position even if the children have no vote, no political power, and no lobbyists. The State is interested in the long-term health of democracy. If it does not side with the fundamental desires and rights of children against the demands of adults—and if it does not side with the natural law of intergenerational development—then it ensures future decline. Hence, when the politicians in Christian nations became involved in regulating marriages, the two rulings that they imposed on marriage were age restrictions and kinship prohibitions. Both of these were about protecting the well-being of children.

The State also has one other interest—the sexual nature of heterosexuals. Heterosexuals have the potential to have children outside of the marital family. This often leads to children being at risk. Thus, the State is interested in encouraging heterosexual marriage because it promotes the core value of fidelity. The aim is to reduce the number of single parents and the risks involved with less-supported children. Because of this reality, Ryan Anderson wrote the following.

> *The State cares about marriage because of marriage's connection with children and its ability to unite children with their mother and father. After all, whenever a baby is born, there is always a mother nearby. This is a fact of reproductive biology. The question for law and culture is whether a father will be involved in the life of that child and, if so, for how long. Marriage increases the odds that a man will be committed both to the children that he helps create and to the woman with whom he does so. Marriage, rightly understood, brings together the two halves of humanity (male and female) in a monogamous relationship. Husband and wife pledge to each other to be faithful by vows of permanence and exclusivity. Marriage provides children with a relationship with the man and the woman who made them.*

Marriage is a natural responsibility for those who wish to create a new life. There is nothing political here. If political representatives wish to involve themselves, their thinking has to embody thoughts such as how they might best support those who have chosen the marital-family norm as a means to fulfill their responsibility to the children they bring into the world. If the State does this, the future is assured.

Such thinking also applies to the other essential elements that make up the social fabric. The fundamental thought to remember is, "How the social fabric upholds the natural rights of the child will determine the future well-being of the nation."

All this is well and good. However, once one understands the above, one can start to see that W. Europe and the U.S. have, long ago, left behind the tradition that expects legislators to protect the natural rights of the child for the sake of future social well-being. Long ago, legislators took the view that it was wholly acceptable to harm the well-being of children to solve the problems of adults. Politicians and judges have deemed it tolerable that adults might solve various challenging situations without personal development taking place. Instead, the adults can now pass their pain or difficulty onto the child, who will then, more than likely, experience lineage decay in their own life. In essence, to fulfill adult desires, many laws exist today that give adults extra rights—the political right to take away the natural rights of the child. Many a politician has come to believe that they have the authority to say to a child, "You have to have a more difficult life just because I say so."

It is useful to understand this concept in another form. For example, slavery laws followed this same dynamic. Slave owners were given extra political rights, and other citizens suffered more as a result. Long ago, we decided that such political behavior was below our dignity. However, today, the law books are full of similarly formed laws. The young cannot complain, and thus politicians get away with passing laws that harm them. If the legislation directly hurt various groups of adults, there would be outrage.

Today, in our "advanced civilization," legislation, or a lack of needed legislation, causes some 50 percent of children to suffer worse life-outcomes than they would have experienced some seventy years ago. Instead of seeking human growth and pursuing excellence to solve social problems, post-Christian W. Europe and America do the following cruel things to their children.

Abortion

There is the social issue of the unwanted child in the womb. Legislators had three choices. They could ensure that the young were taught how human sexuality can achieve the most wondrous outcome—the creation of a precious new life. The young could be taught about how their sexuality has the potential to bring about immense social harm and also bring joy and social sustenance. Surrounded by the right form of cultural support, ever-fewer unwanted children would have been created. Humans would have learned to treat each other more respectfully. Alternatively, the politicians could have left things as they were. Some back-street abortions would have taken place. More babies would have been adopted, or many men would have done the honorable thing and married the mothers to protect their child. Social development would have still occurred, as happened over the last several centuries.

Instead of the above, in the name of "compassion" for the women involved, we accepted the legal killing of the innocent child—some 140 million so far in W. Europe and America—the whole of the population of Germany and France combined. The politicians deemed that they had the power to take away the child's natural and equal right to life.

In leaving behind the Biblical view that sees each person as a child of God with equal rights, we also lost our understanding of our species norm. Today, in our schools, we do not make it clear that we are a truelove species and that, for our species, there are serious complications involved with "free sex." We do not clarify all the adverse outcomes of out-of-wedlock sex. We would rather kill a child than teach students the truth.

In having an abortion, many women experience an attachment trauma, and thus lineage decay is a heightened possibility. A loss of honor for both men and women accompanies the killing of an innocent. In such a space, women start to act less honorably and find it harder to find honorable men. This ultimately makes it harder for both sexes to marry and stay married. With the breakdown of the family that follows, single parenting rises—which is what has happened ever since abortion laws were first introduced. Children with attachment traumas now fill many a fractured community and our jails.

Imagine that we decided it was legally acceptable to kill off our "unwanted elderly parents," even if they did not wish to be killed. Would we see ourselves as building a nobler nation or as entering into a form of barbarism? In killing the child with drugs and metal instruments, many communities become infected with drug abuse and the harming of others with metal instruments. How one treats the child, so will be the future of one's nation.

No-Fault Divorce

There is the issue of the husband or wife who wishes to divorce. In the 1970s, our social representatives had three choices. They could have asked themselves how citizens might be better prepared for the marital and parenting journey. They might have also thought about how legislation might have better supported the marital-family system and the growth and development of married couples. In doing this, today, our nations might see an ever-increasing number of joyful marital-families. Alternatively, they could have left the divorce laws as they were. Western countries had developed despite the problems within marriages. It would be painful to look at some families, but still, community improvement was taking place.

Instead, to satisfy adult desires, politicians introduced more liberal divorce laws. These laws allowed millions of parents to disconnect from their children, and tens of millions of children have suffered attachment traumas and experienced worse lives as a result. Along with abortion laws, divorce legislation ensured the collapse of the social knowledge of our species norm. The financial costs of paying for all the human damage are vast. Even today, when we have so many marriage strengthening books and programs available, we do not even try to offer marriage education or counseling to uphold the child's natural desire for connection, protection, and well-being. We would rather hurt the child than grow.

IVF and Surrogacy

Today, the legislation allows children to be bought and sold in both IVF and surrogacy—all without asking the children if they want to be bought and sold—as we sold slaves some years ago. Again, the law, in a desire to please adults' demands, violates the child's natural rights and desires. If the politicians asked the children if they want to be sold by their mother, they would refuse the offer. The intrinsic attachment trauma that comes with such practices can cause havoc with the child's entire life. Sadly, in IVF and surrogacy, the adults' emotional longing now often becomes the child's enduring emotional pain.

In IVF, a considerable percentage of children end up with disabilities and life-long illnesses—all without asking the children if they wanted such a harmful start to life. Such behavior is against the Nuremberg Code. The Code demands that anyone who might experience adverse effects from a medical procedure must sign a consent form before the intervention can occur.

The above legislation violates all the fundamental rights of the child—their natural right to life, their right and intrinsic desire to know the love of their biological parents, their natural right to protection, their right not to be bought and sold, and their right not to be forced to pay off anyone else's debt. With every right being violated, this creates a social mentality that causes increasing numbers of citizens to become utterly blind to the child's natural rights. Hence, we increasingly feel that we have a right to violate children in new and painful ways.

- Without effective legislation concerning pornography, the natural right of the child is defiled. Many teens today suffer complicated lives because of the degrading behaviors they see on their phones or computers. Today, many addicted young males and females are now incapable of building a lasting relationship.
- Social media channels like SnapChat allow adults to abuse countless naive children.
- Without the protection of a father, tens of thousands of children are now trafficked for sex every year.
- Millions of videos and images now exist online—of adults sexually abusing children.
- In Europe, hundreds of thousands of children have been groomed and raped by Muslim men. The police refused to step in because they felt they would upset some adults.
- In comprehensive sex education—teachers teach our children about same-sex eroticism. If one asked the children if they want to be taught this content, they would say no, but nobody bothers to ask. Also, we do not teach children about the profound risks of such conduct. Many teens experiment with such behavior and end up experiencing more significant risks—diseases, higher rates of rape and abuse, increased rates of drug abuse, and more.
- As unstable cohabitation with children increases, millions of children suffer more problems in their lives.
- We now hastily sterilize underaged, gender-confused children and cut off their penises and breasts. After a few years, most of them wake up to realize they were just temporarily confused and cannot return to an everyday life. Often, a miserable life

awaits. All this is also against the Nuremberg Code, which demands that the subject fully understand the potential adverse effects of any medical intervention. The child is too young to understand what it means to make such a profound mistake. It is our job as adults to look into the research and protect them.

It is utterly impossible to bring about a flourishing future tomorrow when legislative design harms so many children today. It is unbelievable how desensitized we have become to such behaviors.

If you were studying an enduring-love species, maybe puffins, and you saw that many of the males were no longer raising the offspring with the females, that many of the females were kicking their eggs off the cliffs, and that many of the young adults seemed to have no interest in starting a family, and thus the whole colony was going into numerical decline, then, as a researcher, you would be seriously worried. You would be asking yourself, "What is going wrong? What environmental or cultural issues could be causing these behaviors?" You would not think all is well with the puffins. You could not say, "They are building a bright future for their children." You would wonder how long this colony could survive before it collapsed.

What would give you hope that the colony was on the road to recovery? It would be when you saw most of the males and females working together to raise their chicks. It would be when you saw that females were no longer destroying their eggs. It would be when you saw the adults were no longer putting off mating until they were too old to lay any eggs. Then, you would look and see a flourishing colony and know that all is well in their world.

Our humanity is no different. The rules we live by to gain optimal outcomes for our communities are the same. The same fundamental responsibilities need to be fulfilled if we wish for our nations to thrive. The main reasons why so many people today find it harder to live up to the responsibilities that our ancestors took for granted have to do with the type of culture we have created and the expansive, child-harming legislative framework that has been implemented within it.

The flow of energy that built the developed Christian nations followed the motto, "Adults should sacrifice their desires for the sake of child well-being." The current legislation, or lack of thereof, expresses the following unworkable ethos: - "The well-being of the child can be sacrificed to make adults happy." No culture can survive based on such an unnatural flow of energy.

No Marital-Family Norm Leads To No Democracy

As mentioned above, the natural way to look at a community based on puffin ideals is to view each home as a nest where each couple is taking responsibility for their own family. When a nation can be viewed through such a lens, democracy can be born. The core question of the political realm would then be, "How do we keep the marital family strong, thus allowing citizens to be able to take responsibility for their lives, thus allowing our democracy to flourish?"

However, throughout history, democracy has been a rarely achieved experience. It has been hard for nations to come to a point where the social fabric could see the power of a country originating from within the family system. It has been difficult for rulers to relinquish their control to benefit the wider community. Democracies could only naturally occur where citizens chose integrity over corruption, where an education system could help citizens understand how to use the power that they had been given, where the family system was reasonably healthy, and where there was economic dynamism based on free trade and the rule of law. Alternatively, democracies have just been imposed, often on an ill-prepared populace, for example, as they were at the end of the colonial period.

Instead, throughout history, humans have mainly lived under the divine right of kings, queens, emperors, raja, or despots. This controlling form of leadership has similarities with a wolf-pack structure. In a wolf pack, the wolves work together to support the family of the alpha pair. Many of the beta wolves never get to form a family of their own. The beta wolves are kept in their place through the use of fear and aggression. The wolf-pack structure also protects the beta wolves from attack by other wolf-packs. The beta wolves often sacrifice their ability to build a family just to stay alive.

Thus, throughout history, communities of families needed a leader who could organize them when they came under attack. They also needed someone or a community council to create rules and adjudicate when these rules were deemed to be broken. The social fabric was not ready for democracy, but still, certain community-building functions needed to be in place. When the conditions are not right for democracy, royal wolfism seems to be the default way of ordering a nation. The "alpha families" did very well for themselves. How the beta families or individuals were treated had much to do with the quality of the alpha families. These leaders often sent citizens off to war, compelled citizens to build a new city, or taxed them heavily. The citizens often had no right to complain.

When the alpha families were more thoughtful, more freedom was offered, a growing middle class occurred, educational opportunities grew, and society, as a whole, became wealthier.

Britain moved from an aristocratic form of wolfism to democratic puffinism through the strengthening of the marital-family norm from the seventeenth century onwards. In building lasting families, families increasingly became self-sustaining units—with the extended family, friends, and faith community acting as their support system. Each home took on more power, and power slowly drifted away from wealthy families. Levels of education improved. Our ancestors became equals in creating a positive future for their communities. As the natural rights that are intrinsically rooted in our lasting-love norm became increasingly evident, Christian nations brought about the ending of slavery, allowed for the equality of women, and more. All puffins are equal. The social layout resembled communities of self-sufficient albatross nests.

Ideally, even the wealthy should support this vision because it provides for the slow but steady growth of wealth for almost all families.

Today, as the marital family collapses through legislative design, increasing numbers of families need the support of other families through an enforced taxation code. Each time our social representatives claim that they have a right to raise taxes, they take hold of more power. Social energy is leaving the family unit. The power is drifting back into the hands of both elected and non-elected social leaders. As the marital-family norm declines, democratic norms dissipate. One can no longer view the social landscape as being full of puffin families that are capable of finding ways to look after themselves.

Natural Rights And Species Norms

In chapter four, we explored the topic of natural rights. I concluded that since flourishing human communities could only be built when citizens strove to live out the various aspects of our three-blessings species-norm, then all citizens needed freedom to pursue such goals. Thus puffinism, because it gives rise to the idea of equal responsibility, also gives rise to the concept of equal rights. If one looks out across an albatross community, all the birds have an identical obligation to participate in building a flourishing community. No alpha albatrosses are dominating the betas, blocking their way. Hence, democratic ideals are created. However, citizens can only maintain their democracies by choosing to live out the inherent responsibilities that are intrinsic to our species norm. As Father John Courtney Murray once wrote of the American experiment: -

> *It is not an American belief that free government is inevitable, only that it is possible, and that its possibility can be realized only when the people as a whole are inwardly governed by the recognized imperatives of the universal moral law.*

One can look at the American Bill of Rights to see how the founders of America tried hard to infuse their nation with the rights that are inherent in our species norm. There is the natural right to choose the faith community that you feel will best help you through life. There is the right of the individual to protect their own life and home, the right to a fair trial, and the right to protection from an overbearing State. And there are equal rights for people of all skin colors and both genders. And America blossomed under these freedoms because most citizens were trying to use them wisely through taking on Christian norms. Meanwhile, other nations struggled to find energy under various forms of regal wolfism.

What then seems to be the ideal form of government for those who seek to build a flourishing society based on truelove norms? It is probably some form of a democratic republic, like the American system. However, the natural rights of citizens, including children, would be more clearly defined.

Throughout history, most nations have lived under the sub-optimal political structure of royal wolfism. In a wolf pack, to protect their species' well-being, the alpha wolves can attack any beta wolf that they feel is stepping out of line. Thus, very few natural rights are associated with wolfism. Hence, when nations lived under royal wolfism, the citizens typically just had to accept the rights that alpha families granted them. There are no intrinsic natural rights that apply to all citizens. Most political rights are gained through a random series of events but can be taken away again. Because regal wolfism has no sense of equal rights, it has no internal solidity that will allow it to create a world of co-prosperity and peace. There will always be a struggle for equal rights.

In some countries, the norm of another species has also been used to create communities. The Koran gives rise to a worldview that embraces the idea that our natural species norm is close to that of the harem lions. The Koran allows for polygamy. Like the lions, many of the male leaders of the Arabic nations have several wives. Countries that live under the influence of the Koran have proven to be sustainable because, even in polygamy, the children still have their biological parents' daily attention. Other elements of our lasting-love norm are also upheld, for example, staying away from pre-marital sex. There are, of course, many caring and nurturing Muslim families.

However, in nature, the females in the harem species must submit to the rule of the toughest lion around. Gender equality is not built into the substructure of lionism. Thus, the Koran itself struggles to offer men and women equal rights. Because the Koran says that women have half the value of men, women's rights are a complex issue.

Those animals that use the harem norm still have specific responsibilities to uphold if they wish their species to remain healthy. Hence, the Koran does give rise to a vision of some natural rights. These rights form the basis for Sharia law. This legal system has some similarities to Western democratic law. However, in following a different species norm, there will automatically be irreconcilable differences in what might constitute our natural rights.

The most notable differences occur when it comes to the rights of men and women. In Islam, women generally have fewer rights than men. For example, those women who engage in pre-marital sex or infidelity are often liable for severe punishment or even death. These breeches in the species norm are typically blamed on the women, not the men. If a man rapes a woman, the court often believes it to be her fault. Among many other concerns, there are the issues of child brides, female genital mutilation, and honor killings. Also, the rights of non-believers are almost non-existent, as are the rights of those who choose to leave Islam as a faith. Thus lionism, as a worldview, contains no intrinsic natural rights that equally apply to all. Because of this problem, lionism cannot form the basis for a world of peace and co-prosperity. It will always give rise to internal struggles between those who have more rights and those who have less.

In more recent history, due to political activism within the university system, our post-Christian nations have been heading away from democracy towards a new form of wolfism, namely Marxist wolfism. Karl Marx labeled royal wolfism as an oppressive economic system. However, he did not perceive wolfism to be inherently flawed as a way of governing a nation. Marx put forward the idea that if "caring leaders" were in full charge of the social fabric, then some form of an ideal world could be built. In his economic model, Marx contended that many "beta citizens" are wholly incapable of looking after themselves. Hence, they need the support of the pack. Wolves hunt together and share the food around—very egalitarian, very socialist. Marx maintained that the wolf-pack structure was necessary for all beta citizens to have food and a home. However, is this true for humans?

In history, whenever Marxism has been fully applied, it has always turned into a bloodbath, extreme oppression, and social stagnation. Hence, it is good to look at some issues around this well-meaning but deceptive theory.

Marx primarily applied his theory to the arena of the third blessing. In his economic theory, he contrived to develop a plan that would ultimately allow the "caring" activists to take over the running of a nation. However, over the last hundred years, Marxist theory has spread out beyond the arena of third-blessing economics. Today, the methodology that Marx developed to turn a nation towards Marxist wolfism has now been applied to all of the three blessings.

Today, various social movements exist, all of which have used the Marxist game-plan to advance their particular cause. Generic terms are now used to describe these social movements as a whole—post-modernists, progressives, social justice warriors, and cultural Marxists. These movements say that their supporters care about equality, fairness, inclusivity, or social justice. And each chooses a specific group within the social fabric that they say they wish to assist. Thus, Marxism comes across as a caring ideology. The progressives then inform us that each specific group can only be helped through the implementation of their political solution. And their solutions always involve the invention of political rights—rights that are invented out of thin air—rights that have no natural connection to the three-blessings framework.

However, the invention of these political rights always forces the State to take away natural rights from other groups of citizens. Because of this, these other groups suffer harmful consequences they never wanted or asked for. The damage done to these new groups of individuals is always far more detrimental to society than any good that the political solutions achieved. Hence, rather than bring about social progress, Marxist thought-patterns continually cause the social fabric to suffer decay. In the name of compassion and kindness, a nation goes into decline. One must always attempt to see who suffers worse outcomes due to their Marxist-formulated "compassionate" interventions. There is no compassion for those groups who are harmed through political design.

In royal wolfism, the alpha wolves might take away natural rights from citizens for personal gain. On the other hand, Marxist activism takes away natural rights under the deceptive banner of equality, fairness, or tolerance. Their plan is misleading because in inventing rights for a specific group of individuals, the politicians automatically take away the natural rights of others. Rather than having equal rights, as we all have within the three-blessings framework, some groups now have more rights, and others have less. The State is fundamentally saying, "We allow this group of individuals to harm another group, with the full backing of the law." These other groups then become second class citizens. Under the banner of equality, inequality is created. The only place where there is the kind of fairness that will build a flourishing community is within the natural rights that emanate from the three-blessings worldview.

Once one understands the Marxist game-plan, one can see how it played out in the Soviet Union. After the Marxist revolution of 1917, the poor eventually had their lives lifted to a slightly higher level—

having the basics of a concrete apartment and food. However, to achieve this small improvement, the Marxist activists murdered tens of millions of other citizens. The politicians invented a political right to a basic level of living, but, as a result, millions of citizens lost their natural right to life, their savings, and their businesses. Also, when the entrepreneurs and managers were killed off, no one was around to lift the nation to a much higher standard of living. And the lives of many of the remaining citizens lacked meaning and success. Alcoholism and depression were commonplace. The violation of rights caused far more harm than good. Meanwhile, in the West, the poor were automatically being lifted out of poverty in their millions. This happened naturally through the pursuit of excellence and the equal right to pursue one's dreams.

In 1910, it was not so clear what kind of future Marxism would bring about. At that time, Marxist activists might have been excused for their lack of foresight. However, a blood-stained and decaying outcome has occurred everywhere that Marxism has been applied. With its clear history, all today should know this. Thus, today, a Marxist is someone who, to make life a bit better for one group of people, is more than willing to make life worse for many more people. A Marxist is prepared to destroy a nation, to brutally murder, and to harm anyone—just so that they can have power and have an instant feel-good moment at the thought of slightly improving the life of a particular group of citizens.

Today, one can apply this same decaying game-plan to various aspects of the other two blessings.

Hence, in a desire to show compassion for the woman with an unwanted child, the progressives tell us that the fetus must have its tender life extinguished, often brutally. In creating a political right for one group of citizens, another group loses its natural right to life. Where is the compassion for this child? Where are equality and fairness? In abortion law, when natural rights are taken away from the child, then men and women lose honor, single parenting increases, more women end up relying on public finances, and our nations head down the road to bankruptcy. More harm is done than good.

The progressives also inform us that it is caring to allow adults to buy children—as sperm, as eggs, or through surrogacy from their mother's womb. As the child grows, it typically becomes aware of its commodity status. Many of these children experience long-term depression and anger. "Why can't I be held and loved by my biological mother?" "I so desperately want the love of my father." The child might spend their whole life dealing with the negative consequences of their unwanted, soul-harming emotions. Usually, the politically-invented right that offers parenthood to childless adults takes away the child's natural right to be free from slavery. Some two hundred years ago, didn't we agree that buying and selling individuals was inhumane? Where are the child's equal rights? Why does the State feel so concerned about the adults' emotions, but not about the child's life-harming feelings? We don't hear these children's voices because the media refuses to let them be heard. Ultimately, more damage will be done to our communities than good.

And yet again, the progressives want politically-created rights to be given to those who struggle with gender confusion—some 0.005% of the population. In every transgender policy and law, natural rights are automatically taken away from everyone else. For example, in some nations, women have lost their natural right to protection in vulnerable public spaces—for instance, in public showers, prisons, and women's shelters. Men who claim they are women can now enter these private spaces, and levels of abuse rise. Women might also lose their natural right to compete in sports against other, biologically-born women. Women's competitive sports might become obsolete as a result. Why is the State more interested in the feelings of one mentally-disturbed gender-confused male, prioritizing his feelings over the painful emotions of twenty thousand women? A handful of politicians have no natural right to tell all women, "You have to stand naked in front of gender-confused men—men who are still very much attracted to the female form."

There is also the issue of identity politics. For many, identity politics might be defined as political activity that caters to the cultural, ethnic, gender, racial, religious, or social interests that characterize a group identity. However, if I were to summarize what I perceive to be happening, I see the progressives making the case that society should be tolerant of all adults who support the laws that take away the natural rights of the child. Everyone else is an outsider, or an oppressor, or backward-looking. Thus, if you are a person—a woman, a person who experiences same-sex attraction, or an African-American—who wishes to protect the child, you are also an outsider. Hence, at the core of the Marxist drive for power, there is a drive to silence all who refuse to accept that, within the law, child well-being should take second place to adults' desires.

Additionally, the term "white privilege" has been formulated to bring about even more chaos. It is just a re-working of the term "a member of the bourgeoisie." "The whites are blocking others from being successful. We have to make them into social pariahs." If you happen to have friends from every type of background and they all have been able to build a successful life in America, and thus you disagree with the idea of white privilege and say so, you, too, are an outsider.

Support for the identity-politics framework has now come to dominate the hiring process of almost every institution and corporation. Affirmative action is everywhere. Certain groups within the identity politics framework are given priority when applying for jobs. Even within the funding processes of the sciences, applicants often have to show that they have post-modernist credentials, or they will not get funding for their research.

Thus, today, vast swathes of talented individuals are finding it ever-harder to move forward in their professional lives. They are outsiders. Less qualified people are promoted because they support the progressive worldview. The natural right of people to be able to make a living from their talents is now undermined. Economic Marxism is now reborn in a new form. With so much talent being neglected, a nation can only go into decline. In essence, the Marxist demand for diversity and inclusivity is not actually about increasing diversity. All one is doing is creating insiders and outsiders. Privilege for one group of citizens, the progressives, is now substantively being written into the law and into corporate and university policies. Hence, identity politics is purely a smokescreen. It is solely a mechanism to place those who support the Marxist game-plan into positions of power in every social institution. Everyone else is vilified.

It is in these new hiring and funding practices that the Marxist game-plan becomes laid bare. For the sake of feeling good about helping some "oppressed minority" today, the diversity officers of universities and corporations are willing to destroy their nation's academic and industrial foundations. There is no compassion for those who will eventually lose their jobs in industry because less-qualified candidates were hired over far more capable ones. When the universities spiral down the world rankings, many students will underperform in their lives. In pursuing excellence, the whole nation would be lifted up. In the Marxist game-plan, all will be brought down. Certain minorities have been given more rights than everyone else, and the nation as a whole has to suffer the consequences. In bringing a nation down, one is only left with a decimated nation. In this clarity, one can see what the Marxist game-plan is all about. There is no other goal in Marxism other than to bring the nation down. This is the only ethos that Marxism embodies.

It is essential to understand why the core Marxist activists push forward with legislation that looks caring on the surface but which consistently causes ever-increasing amounts of social pain. The goal is always to create lineage decline. Marxist-formulated legislation always creates new groups of harmed citizens. Many of these damaged citizens will struggle to act responsibly, or find it tougher to marry or stay married, or find it harder to feed themselves and their families. In creating lineage decline, ever-increasing numbers of citizens will ask the State, or need the State, to help them manage their lives. The sole purpose of Marxism as an ideology is to bring about a wolf-pack future.

When, due to lineage decline in so many families, the social fabric can no longer sustain democratic norms, the Marxist activists wish to oversee the new world order. They keep control through creating politically-invented rights that harm children and then demonize all those institutions and citizens who disagree. Ultimately, because so many citizens are abused, massive decay is inevitable. Eventually, ever-increasing numbers of citizens will struggle along just above the poverty line—with just enough money so that no significant social unrest occurs. And the Marxist-driven alpha families will be living the good life—while telling everyone, "We are the caring ones. We care about the feelings of these groups of adults." As George Orwell wrote after visiting the USSR, "All animals are equal, but some are more equal than others."

Because the legislative suggestions of the progressives always cause other groups of citizens to suffer worse outcomes, the State increasingly becomes dictatorial. "You have to suffer worse lives, just because we, the politicians and judges, say so." Those who disagree with the laws are increasingly told to keep quiet through hate speech laws. In some countries, if a professional believes that six-year-old girls should not become brides, they might now be accused of Islamophobia. Suppose a teacher says she thinks that the sex-education curriculum in her school is likely to do more harm than good—and she posts her concerns on her private Facebook page. Today, she might well lose her career. The politicians increasingly become the alpha wolves, creating political rights that allow some groups of citizens to harm others, and no professional can say otherwise.

The mentality that gives rise to the idea that natural rights can be taken away from most citizens to express compassion for some other groups of citizens is a complex thought-system that many humans find difficult to fight. We do not like to see families or individuals struggling in life. One of the core thoughts that can slice through all the confusion is, "If natural rights are taken away, future generations will experience worse outcomes, and an authoritarian future will cause them immense harm." Thus, citizens need to understand the puffin-like natural rights that underpin their democracies. If they do not, they can lose them. Hence, it is critical to find healthier solutions to social difficulties—ones that do not take away natural rights.

In a wolf-pack system, most of the beta wolves never get to create families of their own. Beyond just feeding themselves, any surplus economic energy they produce goes into supporting the alpha wolves' family. Today, all post-Christian nations have experienced some eighty years of Marxist-derived social-welfare policies and other child-harming initiatives. As a result, those citizens who experience life at the lower end of the socio-economic spectrum now have only about a 40 percent chance of marrying. This compares to 80 percent just two generations ago. These citizens start to become the beta wolves who never can build a family of their own. The wolf-pack dynamic becomes increasingly evident.

Many of these individuals live lonely lives and have a substantially higher risk of experiencing almost every kind of social problem. Amongst this group of citizens, social issues of nearly every type are continually on the rise—addictions, self-harm, depression, abuse, homelessness, and more. Most of the money that flows through their hands now ends up in the pockets of wealthy citizens, most of whom are married. A wolf-pack dynamic is created, whereby the financial energy of the beta citizens is primarily used to support the alpha families.

Today, most Western universities teach their students to support both this "caring" socialist model and many of the Marxist-formulated child-harming laws that I mentioned above. Then, many get highly paid jobs in the professional fields that seek to pick up the pieces of all the damage that these policies have done to other citizens—child protection services, social workers, lawyers, doctors, and more. A large part of the professional economy exists solely because so much damage is done by undermining our species norm.

Ultimately, a Marxist wolf-pack political structure eventually awaits all nations that do substantial harm to any of the three-blessing paradigms. It awaits all those countries that establish a high-taxation welfare State. It also looms for all nations that forget our marital-family norm and harms so many of their children. It even materializes for all countries that teach complaint, resentment, group-based identity-politics, comprehensive sex-education, and transgenderism to their children. All the above create lineage decline.

It is useful to ask a question. "Once Marxists take charge, what policies might they use to build a healthier nation?" The ones that work for us humans are those that lie within our three-blessings norm. However, Marxism denies all these norms. It denies the validity of a well-run free-market economy. Also, the philosophy works on destroying the family and the sexual standards of our species. Moreover, Marxism encourages resentment and victimhood.

In denying our natural norms, decay is inevitable. There is nothing in Marxism that shows how a healthier future is built. Its sole purpose is to destroy the health and well-being of nations and bring about Marxist wolfism. However, if one refuses to look at the social damage that Marxist policies create, one can quite easily be drawn into supporting their causes. It is so much easier to see the possible instant benefits and not the long-term decline embodied within the legislation.

The core Marxist activists who push forward various "caring" policies today understand this process. They do not care about any of the groups that they say they care about—the poor, women, various racial groupings, the environment, and more. They just wish to use these groups to create more politically-invented rights. Their compassion is false. Politically-invented rights are the only goal.

Lastly, it is useful to explore one last element of Marxist wolfism. Marxist activism always seeks to divide the nation into an "Us against Them" dynamic to gain power. They formulate the deceptive lie, "We are the caring ones who care about a specific group of citizens, and they are the uncaring ones who don't."

In economic Marxism, the deceptive claim is that those who oppose the wolves' policies do not care about the poor. They are irredeemably uncaring. Then, once in power, the wolf leaders have torn the "uncaring" Thems to pieces as if the Thems are a rival wolf pack. How else should one treat such uncaring citizens? This murderous dynamic has occurred everywhere that economic Marxism has been fully applied.

When one sees the extensive damage that all forms of Marxism have created, it becomes evident that Marxist theory was formulated solely as a tool to tear Christian nations down. The historic goal has always been to twist the social narrative. They wish for Christians to be seen as "the uncaring ones." If the wolves can attain this goal, Christianity will decline, and people will increasingly lose their knowledge of our natural three-blessings heritage.

We see how this goal was attained in Russia in 1917. In Russia, many Christians used the three-blessings framework to build successful lives—even if this just meant owning a small farm with only two cows. However, the Marxists could twist the narrative and tell the story that these citizens were only successful because they oppressed others. The Marxists could make it appear that those who sought to live by healthy principles were terrible people. Some Christians believed the Marxist narrative, and others saw the lie. The Marxist storyline split Christianity in two, and, soon afterward, one group of Christians was murdering millions of other citizens from a Christian heritage. Marxism had achieved the task it was designed to achieve.

Today, in America, we see how the cultural Marxists gained this Christianity-dividing weapon on 26th June 2015. This was the day that the Supreme Court decided that no U.S. state could oppose the redefining of marriage. After the Court passed this judgment, the progressives could then create the lie that Christians, in their support for the only form of marriage that protected the child's natural rights, were uncaring and bigoted citizens. The activists could now call the Bible "hate speech." The mainstream media refused to let it be known that most Christians who rejected the judgment did so because the verdict violated children's rights in almost every conceivable way. The concern was for the children and the child-harming verdict. Most Christians are just against any form of legislation that harms children. Just because a pet owner puts their parrot in a cage to protect the parrot from being attacked by the cat does not mean the pet owner is biased against cats. It just means that the owner understands it is their responsibility to protect the vulnerable bird from any form of harm.

In essence, the verdict has created an environment whereby all those who promote the marital norms of our species can now be vilified. This parallels what happened in the USSR, wherein all those who encouraged the only economic model that works for us humans were seen to be selfish oppressors.

Many Christians could now see that millions of viable embryos would ultimately be destroyed due to the massive increase in IVF that followed the Court's decision. Tens of thousands of children would be bought and sold against their natural desires. All these children would lose their natural right to know the love of at least one of their biological parents—and many would suffer heartache and depression as a result. Millions of school children, against their natural desires, would be taught various sexual behaviors that research clearly shows will increase risks and bring substantial harm.

Also, in believing the lie that "Christianity is hate speech," millions of children will walk away from the protection of their faith community and be exposed to many more challenging risks throughout their lives. The Christian worldview and the knowledge of our species norm will increasingly disappear. The damage to millions of citizens' lives will be far worse than the benefit accrued through some 2 percent of the population feeling a little more accepted by society. In essence, the redefining of marriage undermines every one of the primary natural rights of the child, thus locking in place all the previous pieces of child-harming legislation. Social decay will be inevitable.

Here, in the redefining of marriage, the cultural Marxists have gained their Christianity-dividing weapon. There are Christians who cannot see how the verdict harms the child. Instead, they are overwhelmed by the ongoing propaganda that demands compassion, equality, and fairness for adults. Thus, today, almost all major denominations are splitting into two because of the same-sex marriage issue.

The refusal of the mainstream media to highlight the damage to child well-being leads to a one-sided debate. Currently, almost any professional who admits that they are against the redefining of marriage will almost certainly lose their job. The control of the dialogue by the progressives in the media is so thorough that no one can stop the harming of millions of children.

Today, many laws place adult feelings ahead of child well-being. What does this mean about the legislative framework? It means that permanent decay has been built into the cultures of America and W. Europe. These cultures are now under the same Marxist-decaying political framework that brought about stagnation and decline in the USSR. With life getting ever-harder for various groups, citizens will increasingly become rebellious. However, in W. Europe, these rebellions will be crushed, just as they recently were in Catalonia and the yellow-vest protests in France. Authoritarianism is needed to keep such decay in place.

Since all previous versions of Marxism have turned into a bloodbath, one must conclude that this will also be the end fate of all post-Christian nations. Ongoing propaganda will ensure that those Christians who do not think that children should be killed, bought, or sold will one day be deemed as heartless and hateful towards adults. They will be sent off to re-education camps, which might even turn into gulags. And others from a Christian heritage will be doing this to them. In the Marxist-driven black-lives-matter cause, we already see young adults from a Christian background burning down businesses and attacking other citizens from a Christian heritage. This is what Marxist activists have been planning all along.

We are a noble, resourceful species. However, once our political representatives forget this, once they start to invent political rights that violate natural law, they become the new gods. They have designed a new species norm for us to live under. In this dynamic, we are doomed to drift away from being children of God. We become the servants of the political system, and eventually, its slaves. Once separated from our species norm, these politicians can then invent as many rights as they want. This causes the social fabric to be torn asunder as various factions now fight over the kind of species they each perceive us to be.

Today, concerned citizens are being called divisive. Instead, the child-harming legislation causes the social fabric to become a battleground between those who see the damage and those who do not. There is no mid-way position. This divisiveness happened in the USSR, and we, in our post-Christian nations, are heading fast in that direction.

In summarizing the above: -

- The leading progressives want to bring about an authoritarian wolf-pack future. They do not care about your rights or democracy.

- Progressives wish to achieve this future by bringing about some small improvement to some people's lives while, at the same time, harming many others' lives in far worse ways. "The ends justify the means" is a well-worn Marxist saying.
- In each of the Marxist endeavors, natural rights that we all have equal access to are replaced by politically-granted rights. There is no natural basis for these political rights. They can be granted and then taken away on a whim. We all become servants to our political masters and to the media giants who guide the discussion. If you happen to be hurt by the policies, you also increasingly lose the right to say so.
- In the past, left- and right-wing parties mainly discussed issues surrounding the third blessing. However, the Marxist game-plan has now been used to attack all of the foundation stones that support each of the three blessings. Therefore, one can talk about first-blessing, second-blessing, and third-blessing Marxism. Today, one can be a fiscal conservative and favor the redefining of marriage—and not see the profound contradiction that lies within. Finding a political party that supports our species norm becomes almost impossible.
- Marxism embodies no life-enriching principles. In a European and American context, its primary purpose has been to ensure that those from a Christian heritage are killed off or morally destroyed. In the last hundred years, some 200 million have been aborted, some 30 million killed in gulags, and at least another 70 million had their lives radically shortened through alcoholism and drug overdoses—the depressing consequences of both broken families and living in the USSR.
- The terms that the progressives use to advance their causes are specifically chosen because they are hard to do battle with. Who doesn't want social justice? However, once one understands the post-modernists' end goals, one can then see through the fog and deception. In practice, social justice means, "We want to create social injustice." "These people are oppressing you" means "We want to oppress everyone." "Black lives matter" means that, in order to advance our cause, no lives

matter. If you can draw people into believing the lie of white privilege, then you want to replace this with real-life progressive privilege. Those who profess a desire for inclusivity want to include those they wish to include and aggressively ostracize everyone else. "I want to get rid of institutional racism" means "I want the freedom to build racism into laws and policies." All the progressive terms mean the opposite to what you hear.

- History shows us that once Marxists gain power in the name of compassion, you are stuck with their brutal oppressiveness for a long time.
- Today, tremendous social forces are pushing for the progressives' feel-good-now goals. No one wants to be seen to be uncaring towards various groups of adults. Only when some people are willing to express immense courage will we be able to honestly discuss whether it is honorable to sacrifice child well-being for the sake of adult feelings. Only then can we weaken the grip that the progressives currently have on society.

Lastly, along with Marxist wolfism, royal wolfism, and lionism, there is also one other species norm affecting the global village. An ever-increasing number of citizens are taking on the mentality that is associated with single-parent species, for example, the cats. Female cats, like the female polar bears, raise their offspring alone. In today's cultural environment, many men start to act like the males in single-parent species act. The goal is sexual conquest, and then he walks away. Many women also act like the females in single-parent species—hooking up with the endowed male for a brief moment and then separating. The rise of catism leads to a hypersexualized society, which ultimately leads to the harming of the child.*

Despite the rise of catism, this species norm creates no positive social energy for human communities, only decline. There is no male for the female to produce social energy with. Thus, catism causes dynamism to leave the family system and nation. The progressive wolves understand that if they can make citizens believe that we follow the species norms of the cats, then many children will suffer lineage decline and the State will grow in power by the day. Thus, the progressives push forward with catism in the movies and soap operas. They show sexual behaviors that ultimately lead to the harming of children, and they show them as being both wholesome and joyful.

Today, progressive activists have also taken control of the education system in many post-Christian countries. The Marxists in the USSR taught children that the economic norm of our species is like that of the wolves. Today's activists teach children that the sexual norm of our species is like that of the cats. These activists do not care about the potential misery they will cause. They do not care that what they teach is against the desires of most parents—who wish that their children be taught how to live a successful life.

In summary, Marxism is a democracy-ending, nation-destroying thought-system. In this clarity, any publicly-paid professional who claims Marxist leanings should be fired and shunned. It is these activists who should be ostracized by society, not the citizens who believe that child protection should be a natural part of any civilized society.

Today, many East European countries are waking up to the child-harming mindset that has taken over West Europe and America's coastlines. They can see that such a mentality will lead to an impoverished future. So, they are choosing to create a more family-friendly, child-protecting way future. Poland, for example, banned abortions.

Additionally, Poland and Hungary have been developing policies that will help strengthen family life. For example, they understand that when a married woman raises her children at home, she creates socially-beneficial energy that will lead to the continued existence, sustainability, and development of the culture. She needs to be supported. However, the child-harming leaders of West

Europe are not happy with these rebellious nations. They believe they must be punished.

Meanwhile, the UN has lost its fundamental purpose—that of creating a foundation for world peace. Instead, this once noble institution has been infiltrated by unelected activists representing all the different species norms. Thus, it has turned into a battleground between the various species norms—all of which are vying for power. There are Western Marxist wolves—the globalists—who push through all initiatives to harm the child. The Marxist-created, wolf-brained leaders of Maoist China want to expand their territory. The lions of Islam see that the post-Christian nations are in terminal decline because of the harming of the child. Like any robust pride of lions, they also push forward with their goals to expand their territories. And lastly, some factions still tenaciously hold onto our puffin norm.

Meanwhile, in the U.S., explicitly due to forces that were unleashed in the redefining of marriage, there is a major cultural war occurring. The wolf-minded activists have taken control of almost all major social institutions and most of the media. The boards of many large corporations have become infected with the Marxist virus. "We, the caring ones, demand that more children be killed, bought, and sold to make adults happy. This will lead us to a brighter future." In seeing how the American wolves are doing everything they can to destroy the heritage of the trueloves, the Chinese wolves and some of the Islamic lions have joined the attack. If America falls, there will no longer be a worldwide defender of democracy.

If the progressives gain the Presidency, the House, and the Senate in the next election, they will ensure that the Republicans never get back into power again. America will increasingly turn into a replica of the USSR. And the Marxist wolves will increasingly go after those Christians and citizens who still value our three-blessings norm.

In summary, what does the above tell us about natural rights? The natural rights that were built into the American Constitution, the American Bill of Rights, and British common law were derived from the belief that we are a lasting-love species. Only puffinism values the natural rights of men, women, and children—honoring us all as having equal rights as children of God. In the establishment of these democracies, those groups who did not yet have access to equal rights eventually gained them because equal rights are built into the substructure of puffinism. Only the three-blessings worldview offers us a chance to create a world of peace and co-prosperity because only puffinism allows for equal rights.

However, very soon, the whole world might be forced to live under a species norm that is not our biological one. Because very few natural rights are associated with the norms of other species, then authoritarianism will be its core signature. Which one wins will depend on whether citizens of the world wish to act responsibly and uphold our natural, best-outcomes, truelove norms. As in all puffin communities, the well-being of nations depends on whether each individual is willing to take on the responsibility that comes with being a noble citizen.

7. THE ONLY PATH TO WORLD PEACE

The Three Blessings Or Bust

As one looks back in history, one sees a familiar pattern emerging. Citizens become inspired by a religious worldview that encourages men and women to voluntarily take on various elements that are intrinsic to our three-blessings norm. Their nation flourishes and growing numbers of citizens no longer struggle with feeding and housing their families. Art flourishes and great thinkers come to the fore. But, in all that opulence, the culture starts to lose its way. Such is the moment for our post-Christian nations.

Today, we see the ruins of these past civilizations all over the world—the Parthenon in Athens and the Colosseum in Rome. Maybe, in two thousand years, people will travel to see the ruins of St. Paul's in London and St Peter's Basilica in Rome—both built at a time when people were appreciative of the fact that the Christian three-blessings worldview created a multitude of blessings for their families and some protection from the ravages of life. Today, appreciation for this worldview is disappearing fast.

From my perspective, today, we are at a unique moment in human history. As we move towards becoming a connected world, I perceive that various groups are vying to become the ones who will rule over humanity. Islamic lionism and Marxist wolfism are both on the rise because puffins have lost their way. However, to be ruled over is not the puffin way. It is not the place where we, as humans, find ourselves most at home. Because these groups seek to rule, if any of them achieves their goal, humanity will come under the dominion of a species-norm that is not our intrinsic norm. Oppression and appalling outcomes for many future citizens will be the result. We need to find a path away from such a future. And we need to start doing this quickly.

Once one understands such a reality, what hope is there for a world of peace based on co-prosperity and inter-racial harmony?

The only hope lies within the heart and soul of each individual. Only when individuals voluntarily choose to live under our innate norms can our world benefit from the blessings that are inherent in our species norm. We still, as individuals, have to choose to go this way.

One might look at the three-blessings worldview as a constitution that can be written on the heart of each member of the human race. It is not a challenging constitution to remember. Strive to become wholesome and develop your unique gifts so that you have something beneficial to offer your community. Develop yourself so you can build an enduring family and raise children in your loving embrace. Develop your professional skills and use them to improve the lives of others. If we are all the best we can be, the world is the best it can be.

The American constitution is full of puffin norms. Even if the people who wrote it were all flawed individuals, they still decided that all humans were created equal and all have inalienable rights that were bestowed by God. Once the Constitution was agreed upon, the brokenness of society slowly started to be healed. Hundreds of thousands from European descent died to end slavery. Women eventually gained the vote. School segregation ended. Is the U.S. a wholesome nation today? Some aspects are much better than in the past, but some things are worse. I would argue that the main reason for some things getting worse is not the Constitution's fault, but the failure of legislators and judges to apply the Constitution to protect the lives of children. In this failure, lineage decay is setting in.

In other words, even though I am a damaged puffin, if I can seek to embrace the three-blessings worldview and strive for that high ideal, I know that I will be a little bit more wholesome a few years from now than I am today. And if the majority of us can do the same, for sure the world will be markedly more wholesome in the next generation. And, if our children follow suit, who knows what kind of goodness our grandchildren and their communities might embody.

Thus, the three-blessings worldview needs to be embraced by people of every faith and race. It is not just people of faith that need to do this. Individuals from humanistic traditions also need to join in. This is the only solution, or an awful future for humanity will unfold before us.

How can one create a three-blessings movement? One can ask, "When one looks around the world today, which organizations acknowledge that we have a three-blessings norm? Who might unite us in this task?"

In the Christian world, St. Augustine, St. Aquinas, Martin Luther, John Wesley, G.K. Chesterton, and many more have all sought to explain the valuable role that marriage plays in social well-being. The Catholic Church has been teaching many of the core elements of the three-blessings framework for years. And many Catholics have built wonderful families and reputable businesses. Even though the Catholic church, continually, throughout history, keeps drifting away from its essential mission statement, it has proven to have internal dynamics that allow it to renew itself eventually. Thus, despite the significant problems that it currently faces—especially because wolfism has deceived many of the teachers in seminaries and schools—there are always seeds of renewal.

Over ten years ago, the Manhattan Declaration was formulated. The writers intended it to unite all Christians around the marital-norms, as expressed in the Bible. And hundreds of marriage-valuing Christian-based organizations are working tirelessly to protect their nations. CitizenGo, The Family Research Council, The Ruth Institute, The Center for Family and Human Rights, The Marriage

Foundation (UK), and many more are working to protect the Christian foundation. Then, there are always new ones forming, like Thembeforeus, which has caught the fact that the West has created a child-harming culture.

However, from a three-blessings perspective, there are essential weaknesses within the Christian story. From a species perspective, the most glaring challenge is that Jesus was not married. The vast majority of Jesus' words focus on the potential for humans to become wholesome beings, both striving to be free from sin and embodying characteristics that allow us to sense God's presence in us. Thus, though the role modeling of the first blessing is present within Christianity, the modeling of an affectionate, wholesome, puffin-like family is not. The emphasis is often so intensely focused on the disciple's relationship with Jesus that Christianity often struggles to focus on the core purpose of salvation. From a species-norm perspective, individual salvation exists as a means to help people succeed in the arena of the second and third blessings.

Ultimately, the world needs a faith that can guide the believer back to the beginning of the history of humankind. It should seek to start humanity again based on a holistic picture of Adam and Eve, thus role-modeling our species norm. However, very few of Jesus' words explain the inner workings of the second blessing and how two become one so that they can best protect their children and their communities. Also, with Christianity's emphasis on individual salvation, it seems to struggle to come up with a philosophical response that it can use to fight the cultural Marxist's attempt to destroy the marital-family norm.

Thus, despite the goodness in all these Christian-based groups, humanity needs a new movement that will unite people from every racial, religious, and secular background around our species norm. We, humankind as a whole, need to fully claim our species norm and make it the center of our lives. There is a need for people of all faiths to highlight the elements of their scriptures that support our three-blessings norm. There is a need for secular traditions to do the same. At a time when forces are seeking to oppress us under an alien species norm, there is a need to build a movement that draws in people around a shared, life-giving vision. But this can only happen when a certain number of people have come to accept that God or Mother Nature has given us a species norm that works best for us humans. The question is then, "Is there already such a movement in our world?"

This book started out on an entirely different topic. However, in the end, the ideas that finally appeared have much in common with the thoughts in a book that I had read several times previously. When I had earlier read the book's concepts, they were so shortly expressed and somewhat disconnected. Thus, it was hard to see their relevance in the cultural noise I was experiencing. However, when I came to see the larger picture, it became evident that the ideas in that book were succinctly written because the writer just wanted to express the concepts as fact—as fundamentals in the human universe. It was totally up to the reader to do the work needed to find the truth in the ideas presented.

The book I am alluding to is titled *The Divine Principle*. Rev. Sun Myung Moon authored the book in Korea in about 1953. He explains that he received the contents of his book as a series of revelations. The first chapter of his book is titled *The Principle of Creation*. In this chapter, he details what he believes to be the various core principles upon which the universe is built and the foundational principles that allow human societies to flourish. In just a few pages of text, he skims over the three-blessings worldview, the love and beauty dynamic, and the energy systems that are generated when humans unite with their species norm. He also mentions several other core principles.

In the second chapter, Rev. Moon details how, through engaging in immature, out-of-wedlock sex, our first ancestors "fell," and we lost our understanding of our natural species-norm—and thus fundamentally undermined our ability to excel. Most of the rest of his revelation looks at how history has been a process of God trying to get humankind to remember and live its three-blessings, puffin-rich heritage. He wrote his book using the Bible to explain his central thesis. He saw the life and teachings of Jesus, and the lessons embedded in all of the world's religions, as essential steps in this restoration process. According to his writings, all religions are trying to get us back to the same place—back to living our natural species norm.

Eventually, in my writing process, I realized that I was just expanding on some of the central ideas that were presented in his seminal work. It felt like I was being asked to do the work needed—to see if his revelation sincerely offers humanity a way forward towards lasting peace and co-prosperity.

Rev. Moon led a fascinating life. He sincerely believed that in 1936, when he was still a teenager, he met Jesus while deep in prayer. During that encounter, he came to understand that God desired that we live together as one human family, in peace and co-prosperity. He said he sensed God's immense sadness that His children had so far failed to build a human family. He commented that he cried for days on realizing God's sorrowful heart. He sensed someone had to take God's hope and Jesus' foundation and build such a future for humanity.

After he had received his revelation, he studied engineering by day and studiously read the Bible by night. In 1950, he felt ready to start the mission he felt he had been given. He traveled to what is today N. Korea and began to preach in the street. The communist authorities arrested him, bitterly tortured him, demanded he give up his faith, and threw him out into the street to die. Some friends helped him recover, and, as soon as he could, he continued his preaching. He was arrested once again and sent to a death camp. There, he survived for two years in a state of daily hunger while being worked to death.

In 1953, after his release by UN forces, Rev. Moon restarted his mission in the poverty-drenched, war-exhausted nation of South

Korea. He began teaching the three-blessings worldview from his home—a hut made of cardboard boxes. By 1980, he had built a global organization. He brought together people of all faiths and races who sensed that living a three-blessings lifestyle offered the best hope for creating a peaceful and flourishing future for humankind.

One of the core aspects of his movement was the holding of mass weddings. Here, thousands of couples, both young and old, pledged to build marital families that would enhance humanity. After the ceremony, entitled "The Blessing," all couples inherit the title of being "blessed couples." It inspired Rev. Moon immensely when he met couples who had chosen to marry across the racial and religious' divide and then unite their two religious' traditions under the three-blessings framework. The fact that he could encourage young people to take marriage seriously when the rest of the world was going the other way is quite remarkable. His movement was also attacked continuously by those who wished to undermine his vision.

In being at the forefront of his movement, he and his wife took on the title of "True Parents." He wanted to help the world understand that a puffin-like couple was the role model that humanity needed if we were to return to a world of peace and co-prosperity. On numerous occasions, he mentioned that we all should become true parents and that we all should live up to the natural standard of the albatrosses. He never talked about swans, or albatrosses, or puffins. These are just my way of explaining the natural norms of our humanity.

The Blessing vows are simple yet profound.

- As a mature man and woman, do you pledge to realize an eternal true family that will fulfill the ideal of God's creation with absolute fidelity?

- Do you pledge that, centering on True Parents, you will inherit the tradition of living for the sake of others and pass this proud tradition down to your future generations and all humankind?
- Do you pledge that as true parents, you will raise your children to live up to the Will of God, to be sexually abstinent until marriage, and to become responsible leaders who will inherit and maintain the tradition of family unity?
- Do you pledge that you will support all other families and individuals to uplift these ideals—beyond race, religion, culture, and nationality—helping to create the Kingdom of God on Earth and in Heaven?

The movement he built took different names at different times. He first labeled his organization, "The Holy Spirit Association for the Unification of World Christianity," a visionary goal considering the small building he started in. At the time of his death a few years ago, the organization was called The Family Federation for World Peace and Unification (FFWPU). In 2005, Rev. Moon and his wife set up the Universal Peace Federation (UPF). Part of UPF seeks to inspire faiths to work together for the sake of world peace within the context of the three-blessings framework. If they could unite around this paradigm, then Rev. Moon believed that interreligious wars would become a thing of the past. They could then see themselves as being brothers and sisters on a journey towards the same end. Rev. Moon died in 2012 at the age of 92.

One of the essential roles of UPF is to hold conferences that bridge the religious and racial divide. At these conferences, Rev. Moon would typically give a talk. He would often talk about how only true love between men and women can lay the foundation for world peace. In a lighthearted and sincere way, he would regularly encourage the Muslim imams to see the value of only having one wife. He also sought to establish a religious peace council at the UN—a place where spiritual leaders might offer their insights as a means to support today's developmental issues, and also as a way to end inter-religious wars.

Rev. Moon clearly understood the principle of inter-generational improvement through the marital-family system. Thus, he once said: -

> *The most basic characteristics and personality of a human being are derived from his or her family. The family is the beginning point and basis for love, personality, and life.*
>
> *The Principle of Creation is this. Life is born of parental love in the family and is completed through various kinds of love whose stages vary from son and daughter, to couple, to parents, and on to the stage of grandparents. Finally, a human being enters into Heaven, surrounded by the affection of his descendants. Through the family, history and country are born, and the ideal world begins. Without family, there is no meaning to individual existence and no inheritance of lineage. Because human love and life, which are rooted in the family, surpass all institutions and systems, then the family must be the seat of all values and successful ideologies.*

Also, he had seen with his own eyes what might happen to a nation that falsely came to believe that only wise politicians can fix social problems. Thus, in the 1970s, he set up an educational organization titled *Victory over Communism*. This institute educated political leaders the world over. In 1985, four years before the Soviet Union collapsed, he sponsored a sizeable academic conference on the Soviet empire's impending fall. He was almost assassinated for his endeavors.

One of his most determined efforts was to seek the reunification of the two Koreas. He saw that his birthplace, North Korea, was the last place where Marxism still survived in its bitterest form. He believed that if he could help with reunification, this would lay the foundation upon which Marxist-wolfism around the world, in all its different forms, could be now overcome through the teaching of the three-blessings worldview.

In this book, I feel I have been led to answer the question as to whether the three-blessings pathway is the only way for humanity to build a world of peace. After a long journey, I have concluded that Rev. Moon is right. This is the only way we humans will get to this hoped-for dream. We can never build a world of peace if we believe we all have different species norms.

When it comes to the personal application of the three-blessings framework in my own life, I have found it to be incredibly liberating.

It is nice to know who I am and what works best for my wife and I. In embracing the norms of the trueloves, I know I am on solid ground. Through understanding that appreciation is at the core of human well-being, I increasingly sense the miraculous gift of life itself. The deceptive cultural noise slowly disappears.

It is also helpful to know that individuals, if they want, can keep their present faith community and just highlight the truelove norms that are embedded in their revelations.

What does one need to inherit our species norm?

I find it helpful to value and honor the concept of True Parents as an example that I need to follow. I appreciate the fact that Jesus and Rev. and Mrs. Moon helped me find my way through the cultural chatter so that I could build a family that I feel deeply appreciative of. Left to my own devices, I probably would have ended up having children with several women and now look back on my life with a sense of deep regret.

I value the knowledge of the three-blessings framework that guides my life. And I treasure the promise I made with many other couples on my Blessing day, a commitment to live up to the standard of the albatrosses. I would encourage any couple to attend one of the Blessing events. It is good to make a public promise to such an ideal while surrounded by other couples from different races and religious traditions.

How I wish to uphold the three-blessings norm in my life is up to me. I have chosen to learn to teach a range of seminars that look at puffin ways and puffinism. But others run charities, work to create communities of friendship, seek to run their businesses in family-friendly ways, or focus their energy on their children. There is nothing radical here. People of faith and conscience have been doing similar things for generations.

Moreover, it has been useful for me to know other people from a range of different faiths who made that same commitment to puffinism and associate with them to provide a protective community to raise our children in. My wife and I raised our children in a community that consisted of people who came from almost every major religious tradition.

I have also found it useful to read many of the talks that Rev. Moon gave on the art of love within the realm of the puffins.

Today, FFWPU and UPF are headed by Rev. Moon's wife, Mrs. Hak Ja Han Moon. Much of the work of FFWPU has to do with the holding of large blessing ceremonies around the world.

In the spirit that we all should become true parents, able to express the ideal of the three blessings in the way that we feel most comfortable with, two of Rev. Moon's sons have sought to establish their own organizations. Dr. Hyun Jin Moon now leads the Global Peace Association—an association committed to creating organizational and interfaith partnerships centered on his father's vision. His brother, Hyung Jin Moon, appears to be genuinely interested in learning about how one creates spiritual communities where the members can come to drench themselves in the three-blessings worldview. He has established a worldwide collection of churches under the banner of World Peace and Unification Sanctuary. Rev. Moon also believed in the democratization of the ability to give the Blessing. He hoped that the blessed couples could bless their own children and other couples, which is a tradition his sons are furthering.

The organization Rev. and Mrs. Moon established, the Family Federation for World Peace, envisions that a healthier world can only be constructed upon the foundation of small communities working together for a grander dream. To this end, Rev. Moon's vision of how this world would be built entailed the building of communities of blessed families. He labeled these communities "Home Churches." With each family seeking to embody our natural species-norm, power would eventually revert back from the State to the family system. Families would work together to raise their children in communities that are enriched by puffin values. The ideal of becoming true parents would guide their vision. By taking personal responsibility to contribute to community life, many families would be better protected from the many possible risks that life entails.

The ideal of autonomous home churches allows for groups to form around shared interests. Some communities might be more spiritual in nature, others might like to involve themselves in social projects, and yet others might focus on personal development or emotional healing. Once we have embraced our species norm, the ability of different kinds of communities to work together becomes an empowering experience. For example, the communities can support the development of a media organization that can create educational materials to help all communities on their journey.

I felt it necessary to mention the work that Rev. and Mrs. Moon have sought to inspire over the last seventy years. There may be other organizations with similar ideals that are working just as hard. However, does the Universal Peace Federation, or any of the other organizations that have sprung from The Divine Principle, or any other organization in the world today, have the vision and tenacity to unite thousands of different organizations and billions of people together in the quest to create a movement that will give rise to a flourishing world culture? Only history will tell. I only know that with so many powerful movements seeking to cause us to lose sight of our natural norm, those who believe in puffin ways need an umbrella under which they can work together for the benefit of humanity.

If I were to name such an undertaking, I would call it *The Three-Blessings Movement*. It would invite people of all faiths and races to sign up to create a movement based on the following principles.

I, who follow the honorable norms of the truelove species, do affirm the following as a means to build a world of peace and co-prosperity.

I will consistently strive to become more fruitful.

- I pledge to recognize, appreciate, and honor the essential behaviors, core values, traditions, and attitudes that kept our communities resilient and vigorous in previous generations.
- I pledge to take responsibility to set myself on a path that leads to ongoing growth and mastery—in my personal life, my family life, and my career.
- I pledge to uphold the natural rights of all citizens, children included.
- I honor the right of every person to search for truth.

I will consistently strive to honor our truelove, monogamous, marital-family norm.

- I fully acknowledge the crucial roles that the marital promise, fidelity, staying away from out-of-wedlock sex, the expression of ongoing affection, and growth rather than divorce play in the well-being of our children and our communities.
- I pledge to strive to become a true parent who can nurture and protect the children I help bring into this world.

I will honor the economic principles that are embodied within our three-blessings norm.

- I will value the importance of integrity—in my own life, in the legal system, in business, and in the lives of our social representatives.
- I will honor the right of individuals and companies to keep the vast majority of the money that their abilities and skills create.
- I will seek to encourage our political representatives to stay inside their natural remit of protecting, nurturing, and the sensible running of the social fabric, and to pursue excellence as a means to solve social issues.
- I will seek to ensure, in my multiple roles in life, to strive to protect the eco-system that feeds and nurtures us.

Thus, no matter what others are doing, we still all have an individual decision to make. Do we wish to become loyal to an idea that encourages us all, no matter our heritage, to adopt a vision that has the best hope of creating a peaceful, prosperous future for all of humankind? This would mean that we would have to drop various practices and traditions that we currently uphold. Instead, we would refocus our hearts of minds on a new worldview that would bring about a peaceful, prosperous future for humanity as a whole. It is really up to each of us to decide. The Manhattan Declaration asks each of us to determine which side we are going to stand on.

> *Because the sanctity of human life, the dignity of marriage as a union of husband and wife, and the freedom of conscience and religion are foundational principles of justice and the common good, we are compelled by our Christian faith to speak and act in their defense... We pledge to each other, and to our fellow believers, that no power on earth, be it cultural or political, will intimidate us into silence or acquiescence.*

One Day, We Will Work It Out

I would like to take one of Prof. Jordon Peterson's lists and adapt it for my own purposes. I might make the following suggestions.

- A healthy democracy is built upon the wholesomeness of countless individual citizens. The more wholesome each citizen strives to be, the more vigorous the nation. This being so, strive to develop cultures and school systems that raise more wholesome young adults. Thus, they are better prepared for both marriage and work.
- A peaceful social fabric is preferable to isolation or war. In consequence, society justly and rightly demands some sacrifice of individual impulses and idiosyncrasy. This being so, strive to build a culture that encourages young adults to delay sexual activity until marriage.
- Strive to educate all citizens about the species norm that we are bound by so that as many as possible can freely choose to live by the natural laws that guide us towards a more hopeful future. It is nobler to teach young people about responsibilities than about rights.
- Strive to stop our political representatives from passing any law that undermines our natural species norms.
- Citizens have the inalienable right to benefit from the result of their own honest labor. Because of this, strive to build a free market system that, at the same time, keeps the planet sustainable for future generations. Hierarchies of competence are desirable and should be promoted. People should be paid so that they are able and willing to perform socially useful and helpful duties.
- Because nations still live under different species norms with varying systems of values, borders are reasonable. Likewise, limits on immigration are reasonable.
- It is better to do what everyone has always done to build a culture unless you have some extraordinarily valid reason to do otherwise.
- The government, local and distant, should leave people to their own devices as much as possible.
- We should judge our political system in comparison to other, actual, political systems and not to hypothetical utopias.

Understanding what we now understand, one sincerely has to have hope. Today, we can have confidence because we have all the educational tools and knowledge needed to build reasonably loving marital-families. These tools and this knowledge never existed before. Thus, if we can get past the current hurdle and find a common purpose under the banner of the three-blessings framework, then we have the potential to create ever-improving communities. We have enough knowledge to stop going down dead-end streets and start the long, inter-generational process of really learning the art of loving well. We need to tap into our hidden potential and make it happen. Our natural-family norms will always be our family norms. One day we will work it out.

When it comes to raising our children, we follow the norms of the truelove species. We are not walruses. We do not get turned on by watching two guys fight each other so that the winner can have sex with ten women—who then live with him for a year or two. We are not crocodiles. We do not get excited by the idea of watching a woman have twenty children, all without a husband being there to help raise the kids. We do, however, cry in movies where the boy finally meets the girl of his dreams. And we do cry when we read a novel where a child is snatched from its biological parents, and the parents go through the nightmare of trying to get their child back. These things touch us. We follow the norms of the truelove, marital-family species. Our natural-family norms will always be our norms. One day we will work it out.

Like a romantic couple in a restaurant, lovebirds will feed each other to express their deep bonds of togetherness. The truelove rockhopper penguins gently preen and massage each other for the sake of lasting love. The male arctic tern will occasionally bring his soul mate a fish as a sign of his ongoing commitment to "his wife." When the female prairie vole exhibits signs of stress, her truelove partner will come close and show empathy—comforting his partner, "listening" to her, until she calms down.

The bald eagles show us that chasing after one's intended partner out in the countryside heightens one's sense of togetherness. The truelove whooping cranes regularly dance with each other with energy, passion, and joy. The deeply-bonded albatross partners squawk with glee and rub their beaks together in excitement whenever they meet each other after being separated. They then snuggle up next to each other and know that life is good.

Millions of couples have already found that life-long tenderness and affection can only consistently come about when they both respect their sexual and marital norms to a high degree of integrity. One day, many other couples will also work this out.

As humanity, I believe that we do not have much longer to reconnect with our inherent species norm. However, as the philosopher Ivan Illich once wrote, it is a story that we need to get better at telling.

> *Neither revolution nor reformation can ultimately change society. Rather, you must tell a new powerful tale, one so persuasive that it sweeps away the old myths and becomes the preferred story, one so inclusive that it gathers all the bits of our past and our present into a coherent whole, one that even shines some light into the future so that we can take the next step... If you want to change a society, then you have to tell an alternative story.*

CPSIA information can be obtained
at www.ICGtesting.com
Printed in the USA
BVHW041122031120
592418BV00009BA/389